Gre

Act... Create... Be...

EXPLORING
THE
ICEBERG

PAUL LAMB

BALBOA.
PRESS
A DIVISION OF HAY HOUSE

ISBN: 978-1-4525-6314-5 (sc)
ISBN: 978-1-4525-6315-2 (hc)
ISBN: 978-1-4525-6313-8 (e)

Library of Congress Control Number: 2012921510

Balboa Press books may be ordered through booksellers or by contacting:

Balboa Press
A Division of Hay House
1663 Liberty Drive
Bloomington, IN 47403
www.balboapress.com
1-(877) 407-4847

Printed in the United States of America

Balboa Press rev. date: 01/17/2013

DEDICATION

This Book is Dedicated to —

My kids,

Silas and Tyson

My siblings,

Peter, Beverly and Scott

and

my parents,

Eileen and Ewart

Acknowlegements

I would like to thank:

You: because you are looking at this book and, perhaps, even reading it. You are invited to keep this book by your side and to keep it from collecting dust to frequently use the Iceberg Strategies

Everyone I have met, for I have learned well from all

Steve de Shazer and Insoo Kim Berg: for their Solution Focused work

Carl Gustav Jung: for his typology and creative insights on humanity

Katherine C. Briggs and Isabel Briggs Myers: for introducing the Myers-Briggs Type Indicator to us, and enabling all to understand a person's Jungian type

Susan Jeffers: for Feeling the Fear and Doing It Anyway

Debbie Ford: for asking the Right Questions

Staff of the Acquired Brain Injury Clinic, Chedoke Hospital, and Outreach Program, Lucy and Justine

The many people who assisted with this book

Denis Waitley: from the beginning

Daniel Quinn: for Ishmael, The Story of B, and My Ishmael, A Sequel

Delta Hotels Corporation, Particularly Delta, St. John's Newfoundland, Canada

Contents

FORWARD

I had the privilege to be part of Paul's rehabilitation team as he transitioned through stages of recovery and back into previous life roles. Recovery from an acquired brain injury is frequently long and tedious, painful both physically and emotionally and fraught with disappointments, losses and just more hard work day after day. Recovery from a brain injury doesn't take a break, doesn't have weekends off and continues in varying degrees throughout the lifetime of an individual.

Some individuals progress along this continuum more successfully than others. Paul is one such individual. Several factors played a part in his recovery, but the key factor was Paul's persistent optimism and positive approach to the task at hand. Sure, he had setbacks, many in fact, but in each of these Paul would look for the meaning and purpose and inevitably come back to the reasoning that his injury had to be for a reason and he was going to maximize that opportunity. This a man who at one point was comatose with multiple physical and cognitive injuries. For many years now, he has lived independently, continued to be an involved parent and family member, returned to his previous career and at the same time developed a writing career - hence this book.

In this book, you will find knowledge, strategies and suggested pathways to maximize individual strengths and talents and use them more productively in your personal life as well as in your work life. Paul is a living example of being one's own agent of change. He could have decided to let fate determine his pathway, but instead decided to maximize his potential by drawing upon his previous skills and using that ever present optimism he was able to fuel his life goals.

Paul's approach to getting the most out of life is special. Not everyone has it - but everyone should try to obtain it - please read on.

Lucy Wadas
Clinical Manager
Acquired Brain Injury Program

THE AUTHOR'S NOTES

An intent of this book is the motto of the publishing company, Dinner With Two:

Read...Talk...Share.

The motto comes out of the traditional dinnertime that was for family gathering talk and sharing about 'life's' events. Parents and kids would share, or try to get a word in edge wise in large families – like learning the boarding house reach.

Read...Talk...Share.

I am extremely happy for two reasons I will share. Firstly, I am ecstatic and overjoyed (read passionate) being here on earth and as functional as I am. However, I am now convinced that any level of function would not keep me down. Secondly, I'm enthusiastic and overjoyed (read passionate) about life in general and about my life specifically, that has convinced me that what I taught and teach works. This gives me value.

This book, foundationally, is about self-esteem. Coming out of my coma at mid-life like a six year old, my self-esteem, confidence and self-worth was non-existent, lower than a snake's belly. My self-esteemed emerged from my Iceberg Strategies.

This book shares a process I used to move from despair to repair and then to thrive. I describe the traumatic injury that was out of my control that happened to me. As a turning point, the trauma changed and influenced my life. This book describes my choice points. It is a compelling story.

Exploring the Iceberg is a metaphor for life. Many people know themselves only as much as the tip of the iceberg. People are very complex and it is hard and time consuming to be fully self-aware. We think we know others so well but do we know ourselves -- deeply? It is sometimes the most frightening discovery – knowing ourselves deeply?

I have grown up thinking I'm normal and not extra special. Now I know we are all special because we are individuals and are different from each other. It is our differences that give the world strength.

My concern is that people would read arrogance into my book rather than genuineness. My lofty goal is for everyone to thrive, as that is truly possible.

Exploring The Iceberg combines theory with application. I was and am a motivational author, consultant and teacher for personal and organizational growth. I believed what I talked about and was completely genuine. Now I know it was believable because I used the Iceberg Strategies to get to be who and where I am today. I lived and am living the book. Now, I am able to walk the talk. Growing out of my trauma, through my Iceberg Strategies enhanced my value when I had none.

Emerging from the Iceberg Strategies is self-esteem, strength, wisdom and truthful eyes.

In this book the word 'organization' can mean your workplace, your family, your life or all independently or collectively – it's your choice.

I have been given a second chance in life. I want to use this second chance optimally, and I so desire to share with you what

I know and have confirmed by living the Iceberg Strategies. I am no stronger or courageous than you. Each of us has the same strength to deal with our pound-of-dirt - when we are surrounded by life's nastiness.

Paul Lamb

PRLs of Wisdom*

Viktor E. Frankl said,

'Ask not what life can do for you but what you can do for life'.

*PRLs- Paul R. Lamb - Pearls of Wisdom.
Thoughts I place in my heart, mind, and soul. . .

xix

MISSION

Elevate your bar of survival.

STRIVE TO THRIVE!!!

STRIVE TO THRIVE

I

THE STORY OF
THE INVITATION

One

Me
The Happening

Shattering trauma put me into a coma for almost a month. When I came to I was a low functioning adult, like a six year old. Through my Iceberg Strategies I found strength to champion over my challenges and previous traumatic devastation impacting m mind, body and soul. I had to recreate and am rebuilding myself from this trauma.

I was a passenger in a car crash in 1996. I was in a coma for almost a month. Physicians gave me a 3% chance of survival. There is a Glasgow Coma Scale that measures the severity of a coma. The range of the scale is 1-15. A coma is considered catastrophic by insurance companies when it is below 9. When it falls below 3 physicians provide no hope of living. On the Glasgow Coma Scale, I was a 4.

The prognosis at the time of the accident was that if I *did* survive, I would be totally dependent. My injury was categorized as a Severe

Traumatic Brain Injury. My head and face were an unsightly mess and I was worse on the inside. I lost my memory. I couldn't smell, taste, hear, see, or feel. I was unable to walk. I was in a wheel chair. I lost my marriage after a 25-year partnership. I wanted to commit suicide.

I am currently living with an Acquired Brain Injury (ABI) (see Appendix I).

Does the question come to your mind: 'What has a story about the author have to do with me, my profession, or my organization?'

My story enables me to put genuine truth and faith into what the book is about – Strive to Thrive. It is a story that merges my skills, knowledge and abilities as a personal and organizational consultant and teacher with what happened to me. It is a story of being less than nothing and still rising up to thrive. It is a story to provide strategies for you to grow no matter how desperate your situation.

It is a story about how you can rise up when these strategies are put into practice by you.

I am an expert on Exploring the Iceberg because I have lived the book. My traumatic event made me an expert at what I had learned and taught. I became the expert of surviving and thriving from my sudden traumatic events and life changes.

Rising above situations is best done by you. Everyone can rise above life altering circumstances especially by using the information provided. You can enable yourself to make visible your invisible Favourable Junctures knowing yourself deeply. This book is an articulation of how I recovered, survived and thrived, and how you can do the same.

PRLs of Wisdom*

Exploring the Iceberg is <u>the</u> metaphor for life…

Two

The Invitation

This book is for individuals, partners, families and organizations to become more self-aware and thrive in the process. The term, "family" could be substituted for organization. Here it is referred to as your workplace or place of business. In today's culture and society organizations and families have strong alignment. We spend much time, effort, success and tremendous exasperation over organizations, families and ourselves. Organizations take up much space in our lives. Your organization and you spend more time together than your relational partner - so make your organization a great one and your organization will make you a great partner. Know yourself deeply to enhance yourself and your relationship.

Most things in life are relative. There are people that have been through situations that are different than mine. If there is a measuring scale of circumstances that goes from heaven to hell then my story lies somewhere between the two extremes. Some have stories closer to heaven than you or me. Some have stories closer to hell.

In my career I have been immersed in consulting on personal and organizational growth since 1989. In my career and life I used to *talk* the talk. The eventful trauma and the work that recovery demanded is a gift that has allowed me to *walk* the talk. Now I am living proof that the talk is believable.

Delving deep into who you are enables you to broaden your foundation to emerge your self-esteem from the three levels of Iceberg Strategies, below, and enable you to explore your:

The Tip

- *Zone of Comfort*

- *Venting Valve and the 80/20 Rule*

- *Magnification*

The Surface

- *Thinking and Language*

- *Black and White Thinking*

- *P.E.P. Talk*

The Depths

- *Life Balance*

- *Attitude/Choice*

- *Jungian Personalities through Myers-Briggs*

Learning is a life-long journey, not a destination. It is truly a never-ending story.

Exploring the Iceberg is the metaphor for life. An iceberg is $7/8$ below the surface of the water. Many or most people know about themselves and organizations at the tip of the iceberg, rather than exploring most of it below the surface. Exploring The Iceberg is learning, growing, and the journey of becoming completely self-aware. Is this not often a scary process? However, if we do not learn, we do not grow, and we risk losing ourselves in mediocrity. Learn about yourself to go beyond competition...

...Explore the Iceberg.

This book is credible only now. Writing this book before was possible but without personal proof. The book being credible to me is a core value I hold on to, enabling myself morally and ethically to write it. I have merged my life's events with my skills, knowledge and abilities. Now, I bring:

- **Genuine truth**

- **Value**

- **Time well spent for you, the reader.**

Do you want to thrive?

Exploring the Iceberg through the strategies supplied enable you to go deeper with self-knowledge to:

- Emerge your **Self-esteem**

- Create a prosperous **Attitude**

- Increase your life **Choices**

- Discover your **Favourable Junctures**

- Be your own **Hero**

Making yourself stronger and wiser enables you to help strengthen others with out fear of reprisals or handling reprisals with strength and wisdom, which makes you stronger and wise – through a Circle Vision Attitude (what is good for me is good for you and what is good for you is good for me) creating Synergistic Enhancement.

Round and round and round it goes
Where it stops nobody knows.

THE INVITATION

An invitation is extended to all

to use the enclosed information and

elevate your bar of survival —

STRIVE TO THRIVE!!!

PRLs of Wisdom*

Ralph Waldo Emerson said,

"What lies behind us and what lies before us are tiny matters compared to what lies within us."

II

Who I Was

and

Who I Am Now

STRIVE
TO
THRIVE

PRLs OF WISDOM*

Francis Bacon said,

'Be so true to thyself as though be not false to others.'

ONE

PAUL - B.C.

This will paint a brief picture of me B.C. – Before Coma. This provides a dichotomous picture of where I was compared to where I am now.

As the character of Jimmy Cagney said in the movie White Heat – 'I'm on top of the world, ma!'

By 1996, I believed I was at a pinnacle of my life and career. I had the world by the hemispheres. I had great kids, I knew what I was doing and where I was going in life and happily married; or so I presumed.

I had a professional wife, whom I loved. Family is a core value of mine with a foundation of loyalty. I was also the structural parent in the family providing guidelines and boundaries for the children. The kids called the guidelines and boundaries 'rules'.

Work, Marriage and Family

In the mid 1970's, I graduated from University of Guelph in human geography to enter into a career of town planning. After university, I was hired by a small private consulting firm with big dreams. I stayed there for a few years.

My girlfriend of five years at the time was at the University of Western Ontario in Speech Pathology. We discussed her future and she advised me she wanted 'more'. I suggested a career as a physician and encouraged her to apply to Hamilton's university, McMaster Medical School. That is what happened. Because of her move from London to Hamilton, our distance from each other shrank and we decided to be married after her move. I searched for a house to rent and so our plans happened.

After my stint in town planning I returned to university to do some continuing education. Being married to a medical student, however, needed my attention to a full time job to maintain the house, buy my wife a car and help with the government loans for medical school.

As a summer student, I worked in Medical and Forensic Pathology as a Pathologist's Assistant. With people leaving, I stayed in this position for six years.

We decided to have kids. We sallied forth with two boys, Silas and Tyson, two years and two days apart. When Tyson was born I stayed home to be a house dad. At the time, I tried getting leave with pay but this was impossible as there was no paternity leave then. I quit work to look after my kids.

During that time I volunteered as a probation and parole officer for five years. At that point I was asked to take over as Coordinator of the Volunteers as my predecessor was leaving. This was a paid job that I held for a few years. I then moved out of the community and applied for a job in an institution, a jail, as a Coordinator of Volunteer Programs. I did that for a few years.

I then applied for my current position — consultant with the same provincial ministry of correctional services as with my previous two jobs. I have been in this position the longest.

I was at the top of my career path, so I thought, because of what I was doing in my job. This was a short time before my trauma.

I had been involved in a large project dealing with an assessment of a large work group that was a major part of a change initiative.

I had also been a presenter at an international conference of police — a presentation I called The Psychology of Investigation. That was a great time in front of attendees associated with police around the world.

The best part of the presentation was that my kids were with me. In fact, my oldest son helped with my presentation. As well as being on a stage talking and interacting with the participants, I had a slide show. Being unable to conveniently reach my computer laptop, my oldest son operated it on cue.

My son and I were doing my presentation together. I was proud with my youngest son in the audience. When I asked for volunteers to be part of a demonstration to enhance my points, my youngest son approached the stage. Sadly I had to send him back for fear of the audience believing the demonstration was a forgery!

Routine –
Nutrition and Exercise

I was what some people would call a health nut. I didn't diet or follow any prescribed routine. I followed what I called a food management plan. The idea was to look after me to look after my mind, body and spirit. I believed, and still do, that all three support each other synergistically.

I prepared the meals Monday to Friday. I expected my kids not to be fond of the meals I cooked – too healthy. However, I didn't hear any loud complaints. I made a contract with them when they were youngsters. The contract was to eat three vegetables at dinner; they chose the vegetables. Silas and Tyson stuck with the contract until early teens. They were 12 and 14 when they saw their dad close to death. That ended the contract.

I detailed my food intake with a diary. This happened only for a short time, long enough for me to get a measurement of what I ate. Of course it differed marginally day-to-day. Mostly, it consisted of a routine that would see fat intake maintained at around 10%.

I felt what I made and ate was delicious because it was healthy. It wasn't the food as much as it was the perception of what the food did and was doing for me.

Exercising was to the extreme, perhaps.

I ran long distance. I enjoyed running two cross-country races of 33 kilometres. My goal for the first race was to finish. I did and my bonus was I did not finish last. The next year I ran in the same cross-country event with my goal to beat my time from the previous run. I did. My bonus was I didn't pass out!

I agree that the goals do not sound ambitious; but my rationale is that I set goals to meet them. Success breeds success.

I also rode a mountain bike. Part of that routine was to ride in Vermont in the Green Mountains with my brothers on a three-day weekend. Locally, I enjoyed riding down stairs - outside, of course; up and down rock faces in the escarpment close by; and jumping over logs.

Before my injury, I purchased a road-racing bike with aspirations of entering a triathlon. However, swimming was not a strong point with me. Perhaps a biathlon – biking and running – I could have accomplished. Sometimes my dreams didn't follow the rule - 'success breeds success'.

My past routine is not one I currently follow. I can no longer accomplish what I did before. The symptoms of my injury come into play – such as my high level of fatigue and reduced time management skills. Also, although exercising can revitalize and provide energy, the symptoms of my Acquired Brain Injury obstructed me from being able to return to my past routine.

A Typical Morning Pre-injury

All completed in the morning (usually around five a.m.) early enough to avoid rushing into work, unless circumstances ruled otherwise.

I meditated and prayed, then I rode my bike or ran on the nearby trails, or jumped rope or other aerobics. I often also lifted weights or did callisthenics.

- Meditation/Prayer: 20-30 minutes

- Warm up: about 5 minutes—biking or walking at a medium pace

- Strength: 3 times per week (30-40 minutes)—abs., upper & lower back, biceps, triceps, shoulders & pecs — the type of exercise varied for some muscle groups & non-weight bearing lower back raises for stability

- Cardio: 3-5 times per week (30-40 minutes)—a variation or mix of running, biking, jumping rope or step aerobics. The length of time increased considerably when I trained for long distance cross-country races. The cross-country running was easier on my whole body & mind than running pavement.

Meals

I shopped for my family in health food stores or in the 'healthy' section of other stores. My commitment to low-fat, balanced food was sincere. I loved the food I made.

Breakfast usually consisted of a protein drink blended with fruit. At the time, coffee was out, ginseng tea in. My workplace had a cafeteria that supplied the salad to go with my turkey sandwich on whole wheat brought from home.

Dinner consisted of pasta or lean meat and a few vegetables that always included broccoli. Grazing through the day, however, was my style of eating. I sipped a glass of water during every hour, energized by, at least, one piece of fruit both mid morning and afternoon.

Ahhh!...:

I headed for the nearby trails at least once a weak which was for me active or passive Zen time. Those trails were my walking, running or biking haven.

'Get a Life'!

When people saw or heard about my routine they'd joked with me for not having fun in my life. They even might say with laughter in their voice—"Get...A...Life!" Now I can say quite honestly and genuinely—'I did!'

Two

"'Wha' happen'"

One weekend in August 1996 I was away from home on business. I was consulting with the Ontario Provincial Police in a project where my skills were used as an adult educator and organizational consultant. I was working the night shift with the police officers.

Sunday was a bright and sunny morning after the first night shift. I was having a wonderful breakfast on the patio of the hotel where I was staying. I was wondering if life could get any better.

The month before I had presented at an international conference; and I had consulted on a large organizational project. I felt good about what I was doing; good about who I was; great about my marriage; great about my family. Could life get any better? As was about to become evident, I was an insufferable mess.

Sixteen hours after my last memory, my life took the road less traveled.

The night was clear and warm on this summer season. It was the second night I was observing their work as a 'ride along'. The collision happened after midnight. As I have been told, the police officer, who was driving, and I were traveling on a two lane rural road proceeding urgently to another motor vehicle collision. The car went out of control at a high speed. My side of the car hit and careened off a light standard on the roadside. The car spun around and rolled over and over several times, into the adjacent woods. It landed upside down and so did I. I was unconscious.

When the paramedics arrived they found me unconscious suspended upside down by my seat belt in the front passenger side with the air bag blown.

The paramedics cut me out of the car, and I was stabilized for travel and then rushed to the local hospital. Being upside down prevented me from swallowing my tongue. As it was, I was barely alive, otherwise I would have died.

From the small hospital in Peterborough Ontario, I was air lifted to Sunnybrook Hospital, the main trauma hospital located in Toronto.

Coma overwhelmed me for almost a month. The trauma to my head included posterior fracture of my skull, my brain had a left frontal contusion, cranial and cervical shearing, severe haemorrhaging, I had a closed head wound, facial fractures and lacerations, and my shoulder was almost separated.

When there is a closed head wound the brain swells and has nowhere to move, as the scalp is not lacerated. The brain swells due to trauma and haemorrhaging, it follows the path of least resistance to sneak out. It chooses any part of the skull that has thin bony lining to crack and ooze its way out. My brain selected my eye sockets, as that is where the bone is extremely thin, like an egg, only more flexible. Having worked in pathology in my past and removed several hundred brains, I know the welcoming path of which I speak. Therefore, my left eye was hanging out of its socket pushed out by my brain.

Who knew that I would be in a coma for 3 weeks; be given a three percent chance of living or be an immobile dependent if I did live; have a closed head wound? I would be fighting a fractured skull in three places; have internal brain haemorrhaging; who knew I would have a head that looked like an oversized pumpkin, my face would be lacerated with fractures, and a broken nose, that my left eye would be popping out of its socket, pushed out by blood and brain; who knew I would have a myriad of symptoms as a result of an Acquired Brain Injury.

From the trauma, I couldn't walk. I had to learn how to walk again. I had trouble with my vision and I had severe left-sided weakness that, for example, prevented me from lifting a small can of soup.

I lost fine motor control of my left arm and hand, with a feeling of pins and needles 24/7. I lost my memory, both long and short term. I had to learn how to think, and how to talk. I totally lost my self-esteem, my self-confidence, my self-worth and my self-value.

I lost my family that began 25 years before with dating and marriage.

The diagnosis I was given was a severe traumatic, closed head brain injury. In the extreme, I guess I could have been worse, but could I have been worse without dying?

Three

Coma

I am less than nothing. I am at the limits of life. I am 45 years old. I have a 97 percent chance of dying. I am in a coma.

Being in a coma is like not being born. A coma is being on the border as fools and geniuses are on the border of madness and sanity; as teenagers are on the border of adulthood; as evolution is on the border of fish and fowl; as people are in paradigms of being valuable and worthless.

Being in a coma is like being in a vacuum. It is easy to describe a coma like 'nothing' being here; because, nothing is here. But more importantly, I don't even know that nothing is here. I am less than nothing. I am neither dead nor alive. In a coma I 'am' and 'I am not'. [Alive, I was maturely responsible to be on my own. I never knew the meaning of 'being on my own' until coma overcame me – alone, with no one next door, or on the telephone or on email.]

I am alone…

There is no rope to hang on to. There is no net under me to break my fall. There is no family, friend, or stranger to yell to for help. I am on my own. Life has no meaning to me. Life is dispensable. I am dispensable. And this matters not to me, right now. In fact, there is no consideration of dispensability.

I am in a zone that is neither here nor there -- up or down or in between. I am in a place where many fear to tread. But, here in coma, I am not afraid. I have no fear in my coma or of my coma and so no fear has impact. I am so far removed from fear right now, there is no distance. Fear has no meaning in my coma.

My past life, now, has no meaning partly because I don't know of my past life. However, I know I want to go back rather than to stay.

If I return, I don't know what kind of life lay ahead of me, if any. In coma, I don't know the life I had before. I do not know what lay before me:

- *Any heart breaks*

- *Any intense work to recover and rehabilitate*

- *Any challenges and work that lay before me, knowing nothing of:*

- *Persevering*

- *Effort*

- *Patience*

While in coma, these notions and thinking are not even in my mind. There is an overwhelming sense of knowing everything I need to know at this time. There is an overwhelming sense of comfort and safety.

However, I want and need to go back. A part of me wants to stay. I want to go beyond. I am beckoned to stay by a large, unseen, quiet and discrete presence within me and beyond me.

Notwithstanding my desire to go beyond coma and leave life, I choose a different path. There is a strong desire within me to go in the direction of life. There is an urge, deep within me. It is the seed of significance that draws me. Long before now, I nurtured and developed the seed of significance. Deep within me, as I am in coma, I have a knowing that there is something significant yet for me to do.

I am unable to explain my thought process to those who are outside my coma because they would not likely understand me. It is not a thought process, as we know it. It is a process that our words are unable to express. It is like describing a colour. I just know that I want and need to return. The seed of 'significance' is blossoming and it is this that pulls me to my destination.

I also know, in my coma, that if I am not allowed to come back then not coming back is the significance I have yet to do. Intuitively, I know that someone will gain significance from my death, perhaps from what I leave behind.

PRLs of Wisdom*

Cicero said:

"Never less lonely than when completely alone."

Scott, My brother –

Excerpt from an interview

"...When we walked into the [hospital] room [to see Paul for the first time], Paul was physically fit from the neck down. But what was astonishing was, from the neck up was a sight...you don't want to see....

We all had faith that Paul's fitness would carry him through, but you also have to deal with a little reality. And that's not easy."

FOUR

DEAD?

I was in a coma for almost a month. The Glasgow Coma Scale measures severity of a coma with a range of 1-15. Insurance companies describe a score below 9 as catastrophic. Below 3 on the Scale, physicians provide little hope for living. On the Glasgow Coma Scale I was a 4.

The physicians gave me a grim 3% chance of survival.

My work place colleagues were told I would probably die. Relatives around the world had their churches pray. However, my siblings and kids never thought for a moment that I would be heaven bound.

Admittedly, there is some fortune in not knowing what is happening, not feeling pain, not being able to think and put things together. With this on my side, there were no thoughts of imminent death or anxieties of being dependent and immobile. There was no fear because my mind was incapacitated by severe trauma. My mind didn't work. I didn't know what fear was!

Who knew that I would soon be in total despair both inside and out? Did I care what happened to me or not? I have no memory of this. I could have been an amoeba and not known or cared. When my brain was finally able to put things together, yes, I *did* think I was an amoeba. I was less than nothing. I wanted to be an amoeba.

Would it have been simpler just to die? From the trauma, I was unsightly on the outside and a mess on the inside.

I was in several different hospitals for seven months. Early on in recovery, I would forget visitors a minute after they left. The injury prevented my brain from accessing the area that held my memory.

The crash didn't kill me, but I thought I might kill myself.

Five

Near Death Experience

This is difficult to write about. Yet, I decided to include it in my book.

I have no memory from 16 hours before the coma until about three months after. I do remember this.

When I awoke while still in my coma (note: not awoke *from* my coma but while *'in* my coma'), I was lying on my back in a hole. Some may identify that, and I will for brevity, as a grave. I was not able to see, while I knew I was lying down. At once I could see, like opening eyes waking from sleep. Looking up from below I saw a fully cloaked figure standing at the 'grave' side. At first I saw the tip of the boot the figure wore and followed it up to the hood of the cloak draping a faceless face.

The feeling within me is indescribable to this day. I can say that I knew everything I needed to know with utmost contentment. This was security, safety, ultimate compassion, caring, and knowing.

How long was I there? Five minutes, one hour, eight days, an eternity? There was no sense for time. I simply knew all I needed to know.

I asked mindfully if I could return and it was as if the figure already knew. It was at that time that I saw a feature on the face of the cloaked and hooded figure. The feature was a smile. This smile was warm, comforting, and knowing - one that I had never seen or felt in my past or ever seen since.

The figure facing me with that smile and an outstretched arm gracefully guided me the way to go out. I could not walk, yet, without effort I arose from the 'grave' and walked, glided out, carrying that contented feeling with me - again, a feeling never felt since.

BEV,
MY SISTER –

Excerpt from an interview

"Paul was in a coma for [almost a month]. When he awoke, I heard him speak for the first time. He said, "Wha' happen'." I said, "You were in a car accident." He said, "How many people did I kill?" I said, "You were the passenger in the car and no one was killed."

… When I looked at Paul, there was deadness in his eyes…. When answering a question Paul had been asked, it seemed the words had to travel a long distance before he spoke…"

Six

Less-Than-Nothing

You know where I was BC – Before Coma. Post coma, memory loss and without being loved, I believed myself to be less-than-nothing.

What I lost:

- Self-esteem

- Self-confidence

- Self-worth

- Self-value

- Identity

- Memory

- Income – from two to one income

- Family home, gone – the home where my children spent their formative years

- Intact family

- Complete fatherhood – my injury stopped me from being the father I desperately wanted to be and had created

- Advanced physical ability – no longer could I do the aerobic and strength building I once did

- Self-control – physically and emotionally – with my emotions rising to the surface

- Informal leadership at my workplace

- Who I was

SEVEN

THE WEST COTTAGE – A WORKING VACATION?

I t was work but it was no vacation at the cottage. The West cottage was the ABI rehabilitation clinic at Chedoke Hospital in Hamilton, Ontario, Canada. This was my new home for six months in the Acquired Brain Injury ambience.

The recovery path had many challenges!

I was confined to a wheelchair, although today I would not use the word "confined". I had severe left sided weakness with my left arm dangling from my shoulder. Planning my movement was no longer habitual but took focus and concentration. Rather than my brain telling me what to do, I had to tell my brain. Nerve and neuron damage impeded control over my muscle and skeletal structure. I had to tell my body parts what to do for me to move. For example, when I was learning to walk – *"OK, leg and foot, move forward and take a step"*.

I had poor balance, low endurance and poor co-ordination. I had severe headaches and muscle weakness that impaired by physiotherapy. I had difficulty concentrating and remembering. My sleep and mood were affected, my senses were diminished and I had numbness in my lips and gums, affecting my teeth.

Today I still have most of these symptoms, to a lesser degree.

I was totally dependent. The Cottage was a time to learn independence. In addition to my physical limitations, I had lost the core of my being. I believed I had no value, dignity or worth. This time at the Cottage was the beginning of regaining the core of my being. There would be baby steps to regain – me. Then there would be a sledgehammer slammed up against me, causing me to lose all the baby steps of progress I had gained and much more.

At age 45, I couldn't look after myself. I needed help from others. I needed help to do everything, everyday. My new friends were an entourage of therapists – a case manager to coordinate my recovery, a psychologist to help me learn how to think; speech therapist to help me talk; a physio therapist to help me get stronger and learn how to walk, if that were to be so; an occupational therapist; a recreational therapist; a rehabilitation therapist; and the physiatrist (a physician specializing in physical medicine and rehabilitation. Physiatrists treat a wide range of problems from sore shoulders to spinal cord injuries).

Hospital staff were there helping me or watching me do everything from getting out of bed into my wheelchair, going to the bathroom, brushing my teeth, taking a shower. They supervised me all day, helped out of my wheel chair getting into my pyjamas then into bed.

My physical strength was weakened by the cervical shearing and from being lifeless in a coma. The physical weaknesses were compounded by the low cognitive function. I had a 1% ability to understand unfamiliar information.

In the morning, I was escorted in my wheelchair into the bathroom. In the bathroom my toiletries were displayed. The staff would have to cue me to use them and initiate what to do next and with what, as simple as brushing my teeth.

'This is a toothbrush. Put toothpaste on the toothbrush and then brush your teeth. Good for you. Now you can...' And so it went.

That would occur every morning until the routine was under my skin so that I would know to do it myself. I didn't know it at the time, like a child but I was learning independence!

Physically, I was in a wheel chair and had a very weak left side (not being able to even lift a can of soup from a table) and loss of balance. Upstairs my brain made me more dysfunctional. As well as my physical limitations, I was worse in the thinking, understanding and organizing departments.

Assessments

The myriad of assessments had a double edge to them. They were helpful for staff to understand the extent of my injury and the progress of recovery. The assessments helped the staff to set goals for me. They were harmful to me, as they tended to have a predominating control feature. In recovery, there is a definite perception, if not reality, that independence and control are gone. Patience may often feel pushed around by assessments, especially when they already feel out of control.

Eight

Memories Are The Corners Of My Mind...

If memories are in the corners of the mind, my corners were rounded by the trauma allowing no place for memories to linger.

I have been told some of the first words I spoke coming out of my coma were - "wha' happen'". I also said - 'Don' le' them pull the plug.' After the stint in my coma and having my brain incapacitated, my speech was stilted, stunted and inarticulate.

I couldn't remember (and still have no memory of this) sixteen hours prior to the crash (retrograde amnesia) and memory loss for about 3 months after the trauma. I know the exact moment my memory wiped out, and I remember the last things I said and did.

I remember finishing breakfast on a gloriously warm and sunny morning. I then walked back to my hotel room for some sleep after an all night 'ride along'. I remember walking by the hotel reception desk and saying 'good morning'. That is it. Then black! Three months later, when my memory began returning it was less definitive; it simply faded in. I still have trouble with pieces of my memory before trauma that I have never recovered. I live some of my past vicariously through my kids and others.

For some things I don't remember I use my past experiences as a foundation to compensate for memory losses. For example, in my past, I did many activities with my kids – hiking, bike riding, playing games, coaching and so on. The accumulation of those experiences provides a sense of remembering activities that are lost in memory. I snuggle into a past activity I do remember and enjoy listening to the story they are telling me even though I don't remember.

Having no memory is like when I was in a coma except my eyes are open, not closed. And having no memory is like the living dead. I have no idea that things were happened with me there or not. I can't remember. Not being able to remember is like being devoid of all my senses. I had no thoughts; I had no emotion, no taste, no feeling and no smell. I had the memory of a goldfish – about one minute.

I have no senses because I can't remember what I experienced. I can't smell the most fragrant flower. I can't see the most beautiful sight that may be before me. I do not have a life. I can have none of these worldly pleasures because I can't remember any of them. I was devoid of all senses and thinking.

Perhaps another way to understand memory and its loss are in these questions. Do you remember when you were born? Do you remember when you were a baby? Do you remember the first thing you saw or understood?

The first thing I remember lying in my rehabilitation hospital bed is staring at the two black dots on the ceiling. They were comforting. They became the only thing familiar to me then. In those days I would lay in bed staring at the dots and think – well, not think, because I couldn't. I would just be. My visitors cared for me but when they left

I couldn't remember they had been there with me. However, the two dots were with me the entire time while I lay in bed.

Then, one day a dot left me - forsaken once again - by a dot!

Do you know how difficult it is to differentiate one dot from two when seeing double and you don't know you're seeing double? Do you know what it's like thinking you see what everyone else sees when they see something different?

I didn't even ask if there was one dot or two. Even if I was aware of my vision problem, and I wasn't, I couldn't piece things together; if I saw double then it didn't come automatically to me that I was seeing two dots when there was one.

That's what I saw! Seeing is believing – right? – wrong!

It was months later when my grey matter seemed to be progressing, that I began to realize that there was only one dot.

I didn't know I was in a hospital or in a rehabilitation centre. I didn't know where I was, or remember how I got there. Who cared, anyway? I didn't know much. I couldn't even think. My brain was numb and incapacitated. I had come out of a three-week coma diagnosed with a severe traumatic brain injury. I was on the precipice of losing my life.

I was also on the precipice of losing my wife.

NINE

AND NOW THIS!?!?
WALLOP!

A sledgehammer slammed up against me. It was during this time of rehabilitation I learned my wife no longer loved me and was on her way out of our 25-year relationship together. Receiving this news from my wife, especially while still in hospital, put a deep gouge into my recovery and rehabilitation progress.

If there were struggles in the relationship I had been unaware of them. I was hit hard and blind-sided like being the passenger in the police car, again.

I was stunned. Once again I fell into a coma - except this coma was different. It involved my heart. However, my mind was overwhelmed and terribly confused.

I was in an out-of-control situation again - partly because I couldn't put thoughts together for me to understand. I had become a simpleton. My heart was telling me something that I didn't want to know.

In my initial three-week coma I felt no pain. Now my heart in a coma felt a tidal wave of hurt, loneliness and abandonment. Twenty-five years gone - snuffed out like a candle – just like my brain had been snuffed out by trauma.

Family has always been a core value for me. I've always considered family as an institutional structure stabilizing the entire social fabric and mine. Losing my intact family was another loss of my core being.

Depression overwhelmed me and fastened me to my recovery bed; I stayed there that night, the next day, the next night and more. Hospital staff was unaware of the shock I heard that night. Presuming my depression resulted from my rehabilitation, for the next few days, one by one the hospital staff attempted to coax me out of bed every day to return to my therapy. They were unaware of my news.

I was sinking into the depths of nothingness once again, like a ball and chain was fastened to my ankle as I swam in the ocean of life.

Eventually, the encouraging talk by each and every hospital staff took hold of my depression and roused me out of bed to return to my physiotherapy. They persevered with individual and group effort. At the time I didn't care. In retrospect, I appreciate their perseverance, effort and patience.

TEN

BLACK AND WHITE THINKING

I had Black and White Thinking. It is also known as absolute thinking or the thinking of teenagers. In Black and White Thinking there is no continuum to life. It is thinking and language that focuses on extremes and prejudices. This type of thinking attaches to mature thinkers when they are overwhelmed by stress or emotions. Extreme thoughts and words are emphasized. Such words as 'always', 'never', 'anymore', 'all' (such as 'all the time') are words that are intrinsic in Black and White Thinking.

My Thoughts at the Time

- *No one loves me, anymore!*

- I can't do *anything anymore!*

- I'm *not anything* like me *at all!*

- I'm *totally* somebody else!

- I don't like *any* of my life!

- I'm *not anything* of the father I once was!

- I'm *losing* my family!

- There's *nothing* to care about I *hate* me!

- I'm *pathetic*!

- I can't walk *anymore*

- I've *lost all* my independence

- I *can never* think straight

- *I've created* a *broken* family for my kids, my dearly beloved wife (who I thought I was going to be with forever) is gone

- I'm *broke* financially

- My life I built is *gone*

- I lost *everything* about me except my life, and what was that worth – *absolutely nothing*!!!

I was depressed knowing my wife no longer loved me that was translated by my Black and White Thinking that nobody loved me. This was exacerbated by my trauma and injury. However, when I redirected my thinking and I focused on my rehabilitation, my depression subsided from knowing my wife no longer loved me. My Black and White Thinking also waned while I was in hospital.

However, when I finally arrived home I was faced with the realities once again of being left.

My depression returned. There was only one solution in my Black and White Thinking. That was to do Black and White Behaviour – kill my injury, kill myself.

Eleven

Energy To Think

I was previously a long distance runner. The activity my brain moves through daily is very much like that.

My brain works with measure. The mind is the most complex and functionally important organ in the human body. If the brain doesn't work then there is no one. The brain processes, thinks, organizes, operates the other organs in the body. In other words, it takes a well full of energy to function when there is no injury. When there is an injury, such as a Traumatic Severe Brain Injury, it takes two wells worth of energy.

Fatigue was huge with me in the early stages of my recovery and still is, especially when or because my brain runs a marathon each day. Everyone tires physically and mentally as the day wears on. For me, my physical and mental exhaustion happens sooner and I am more tired at days' end.

For those who have never run distance another metaphor may be more appropriate. Perhaps you remember as a kid someone would hold you back when you tried to run. They would grab your shirttail and you would run and run and get nowhere fast. Sometimes, that is how my brain feels and works. Sometimes, no matter how hard I try I just can't grasp the idea, or organize my thoughts or see the big picture. My brain is being held by its shirttail.

At times, it seems like my mind is wading through molasses, perhaps as you have experienced when desperately tired.

It seems my brain wants to get it and just can't! My mind gets very frustrated when this happens although today I've learned and continue to learn - to live with it like every other symptom.

III

THE STORY OF THE POUND-OF-DIRT

STRIVE
_TO_
THRIVE

PRLs of Wisdom*

Everyone eats a pound-of-dirt in their life —
some sooner, some later, some throughout…

ONE

THE POUND-OF-DIRT

Are you digesting your pound-of-dirt, yet?

This is the pound-of-dirt everyone eats in their lifetime - some sooner, some later, some throughout – but everyone does. You need to experience one story to appreciate the other. We don't know 'high' unless there is 'low'.

Carl Jung said: "Even a happy life cannot be without a measure of darkness, and the word happy would lose its meaning if it were not balanced by sadness. It is far better to take things as they come along with patience and equanimity."

You choose the definition of your pound-of-dirt. It is unfair to determine or judge another person's dirt. We all have different perceptions and attitudes. As it is said, 'one's garbage is another one's treasure'. One person's nastiness, in the extreme, is another's sublime experience. It's your pound-of-dirt.

Foundationally, and inherent in personal growth, is the notion of - 'appropriate responsibility'. If the term 'growth' is used and there is no appropriate responsibility, then a different word needs to be used. There is no growth without appropriate responsibility. Having the right character is doing something appropriately responsible when no one is watching.

Two

Turning Points And Choice Points

There have been many turning points in my life. There have been many choice points in my life. Turning points often happen when circumstances are out of control. Choice points happen when the circumstance is in control. My traumatic event was out of control. That was a turning point. The circumstance after the trauma was in my control. These were choice points.

Choice points hinge on the 'readiness' to turn. After much denial, I chose my readiness to turn.

There was no failure only feedback. The feedback contributed to and increased my wisdom. What was useful to me in my life and goals I kept; I kept the best and forgot the rest. There is enough time to learn what we need to know rather than enough time to learn everything.

Who am I now?

Some think I'm a better person. Others think I am no longer the same person, changed entirely. Others think I'm the same. The latter thinking may come out of the notion that I am part of the 'walking wounded'. What this refers to is the fact that my injury is hidden as it is inside my skull – my brain – which we do not see.

You do not see the challenges that live upstairs. Being the 'walking wounded' is a great asset and a great liability. As a result of my physical healing from the trauma I looked the same. Looking at me one cannot distinguish any challenges and handicaps. I have learned compensating strategies to keep my symptoms camouflaged.

It is a great liability because the challenges and handicaps cannot be seen. Notwithstanding all my denial, I chose to welcome the trauma in my life. I decided and chose to accept what happened to me. I didn't ask for it to happen. The occurrence was out of my control. I chose not to let that stop me. How did I welcome my out of control trauma? I chose to search for its benefits. Once I welcomed it, I went from "Why did this happen to me?" to "How can I use this to work for me and beyond me?"

It took time, strategies, patience, understanding (by many) and therapy. It did not happen overnight. I went through denial, the stages of grief, and my time with therapists.

If I felt sorry for myself, hung on to the 'Poor me' attitude, let go of the demanding physical work, stayed at home without returning to work, stagnation may have been my destiny.

But I chose another path. I chose to move from despair to repair.

My biggest nightmare is dreaming about where I would be in life and what I would be doing if I hadn't chosen to move from despair to repair! The 'Poor me!' syndrome would have its grasp on me around my throat. It's a nightmare from which I tend to stay away.

It will be your choice to welcome these Iceberg Strategies or not. It will be your choice to use and create your life and your organization to be the best. It will be your choice to let the "poor me" syndrome push you around. Or will you take control and push it away to keep you balancing your life?

The Iceberg Strategies are not esoteric or unique to me. They are strategies that you use already or can use starting now - all or one of them.

The world is handed to you and me. You and I decide and choose if it will be on a silver plate or a plate of coal. That's what we do with what we are handed - welcome it or shun it. Place it on a silver platter or a plate of coal.

I avoid considering myself a survivor. I use different language and it is a word undefined by dictionaries but I know what it means. I consider myself a 'thriver'.

PRLs of Wisdom*

Jiddu Krishnamush said:

"If you trust the river of life, the river of life has an astonishing way of taking care of you.

THREE

MOVING FROM DESPAIR TO REPAIR

My life had taken a one-eighty degree turn. I went from having a good intellect to dealing with a Severe Traumatic Brain Injury. I went from being very active to a wheelchair; from great confidence, high esteem and worth to notions of no value and suicide.

Dealing with my Acquired Brain Injury was one matter. Dealing with the loss of my wife was something else again. Losing my partner of 25 years after losing all my other traumatic losses seemed to be an impossible burden, hence the desire to commit suicide. Furthermore, with my injury, I was unable or mentally incapacitated from dealing with the trauma. I was unable to think the way I wanted to think. What is the point to life? I heard my wife at the time say she no longer loved me. My Black and White Thinking took that to the extreme and told me I wasn't loved by anyone. My confidence and self-esteem were gone. Why live? What is the point? I couldn't figure my life out; I felt the best of my choices and the only choice was suicide.

Other parts of my family, my kids, siblings and parents persevered. They were always there.

I believed myself to be a great disappointment to my family. Although I wasn't, my Black and White Thinking was telling me differently. It is important to be clear. At no time did I hear from my kids, my siblings, my parents or any part of my extended family that I was a disappointment. It all came out of my own Black and White Thinking.

My family's behaviour showed me morals and values that I held onto in my old life. They held a mirror up to my face and I didn't like what I saw. If I committed suicide, I would be the biggest disappointment of all - even more of a disappointment because of who I was and what happened to me.

My moving from despair to repair was a simple task. I simply changed my mind.

Changing my mind was crucial and all-important to the beginnings of the work I yet had to do and the strategies I used. These strategies, I now call Iceberg Strategies, became a part of my life through consulting and teaching them. If you choose to use one or all of them, ingrain them to use naturally and habitually in whatever happens in your life.

Not changing my mind to repair I would still be in despair with no passion create a new Paul of my liking. Having outside support is so valuable. But that outside support of family, friends, and health care workers would have been worthless if I did not *decide* to work at recovery. It was all up to me no matter the outside support I received.

Only when I changed my mind did the work start. The work involved took perseverance, effort and patience.

There is a song by Chumbawumba, Tubthumping that says:

I get knocked down

But I get up again

You're never gonna keep me down

I've played that song over and over on the stereo and in my head!

I now live in a world of choice rather than chance. This is driven by my attitude that keeps me moving forward rather than a 'badittude' that blocks me.

It is time to move forward to talk Exploring the Iceberg moving through your pound-of-dirt with the Iceberg Strategies..

Rising above situations is best done by you. Most people can rise above life-altering circumstances especially by using the Iceberg Strategies.

It is time to examine the strategies I used and use to recover, survive and thrive.

IV

The Story of
The Iceberg
Strategies

STRIVE
TO
THRIVE

PRLS OF WISDOM*

Learning is a life sentence...

ONE

THE FOUNDATIONS

This section talks about how I used the Iceberg Strategies and went from despair to repair. It is also written with you in mind – you, your family, profession, and your organization. My intent is for us to journey together to survive and thrive!

I ask you to keep this book and the material from collecting dust. As said previously, Exploring The Iceberg is a life long journey and very few reach total self-awareness. This is inherent in the Invitation. It is the reason these Iceberg Strategies are foundational. Ingraining strategies is best for thriving, if not surviving. The continuum I have used and still do is –

Good	*Better*	*Best*

With the example of eating a 'pound-of-dirt' situation, it is 'Good' when you use your own ways to digest the 'dirt'; 'Better' if you use your own way adding the Iceberg Strategies ; 'Best' if you ingrain these and your strategies 'pre-pound-of-dirt' time.

I can say this with confidence because all that I had been teaching and consulting I had forgotten. I lost a good chunk of my memory and had to relearn over time after the trauma. My re-learning came to me easier than the first time and quicker because I had ingrained it many years before. Before and over time I had planted the seeds of survival within me. Because I had ingrained them, the seeds of survival blossomed instinctively as I had no wherewithal to tap into them. The seeds of survival blossomed into strategies to operate of their own fruition as I was unable to call upon them myself.

I was overwhelmed and my mind was incapacitated. There are times in each life or in the life of an organization when people get overwhelmed. Thinking becomes muddled and that is when it is taken over by instinct and impulsively instinct becomes our shield or protection. Ingrain the Iceberg Strategies to create and maintain the best organization. Enable yourselves to call upon them or enable them to be put into operation naturally at most times - dealing with difficult people, change and transition, being out of control and any other time when using them is to our advantage and the advantage to those around.

I am still learning. The strategies are listed below and the following chapters will dwell on them. I have described them as separate and distinct strategies. However, they are dynamic and synergistic. Using one strategy is good, using more is better, using them all is best.

In retrospect I used these Strategies to recover, survive and thrive and enhance my passion for life.

The Iceberg Strategies bring out or enhance our strength and courage to help create passion. A life without passion is a life denied.

PRLs of Wisdom*

Socrates said:

"The unexamined life is not worth living for a human being."

Two

The Iceberg Strategies

The Tip

- *Zone of Comfort*
- *Venting Valve and The 80/20 Rule*
- *Magnification*

The Surface

- *Thinking and Language*
- *Black and White Thinking*
- *P.E.P. Talk*

The Depths

- *Balancing Life*
- *Attitude/Choice*
- *Jungian Personalities through Myers-Briggs*

THREE

THE TIP

THE ZONE OF COMFORT

The Zone of Comfort Strategy is at the tip of the Iceberg. The Iceberg Strategies will reach deep inside the Iceberg to the Jungian Personalities through the Myers-Briggs Type Indicator.

I chose to describe the Zone of Comfort firstly as it helps to put the other Strategies into operation more comfortably. Working with these strategies or changing our respective minds is more easily done in the Zone of Comfort. This is a simple and valuable notion that comes from a vast amount of commonsense. I first read about this notion in a book, Feel the Fear and Do It Anyway, by Susan Jeffers. Your Zone of Comfort is the space where you feel yourself to be comfortable, confident and capable to take action and can handle any resulting consequences. This supports the belief in yourself, which is the number one belief in life. It is important to realize that your Zone of Comfort is relative and may be different than another's. What is scary for you or me may be routine for others.

Feeling the fear and doing it anyway is linked to the idea of reasonable risks. If the action you're are taking or considering poses a reasonable risk, then it falls within your Zone of Comfort. After the trauma and early in my recovery, my Zone of Comfort could fit on the head of a pin. I had no comfort, no confidence and no capability - I had no belief in myself. And even though I was in a wheelchair I eventually took the figurative baby steps to increase my Zone of Comfort. Then, I had a very minimal definition of reasonable risk. Without the 3 C's - Comfort, Confidence and Capability - my steps were smaller than baby steps! One example of the baby steps I took is getting myself out of the wheelchair. As mentioned, my off-set balance from the trauma was one symptom that kept me from walking. I did not get out of the wheelchair and suddenly walk! With my additional physical weaknesses as well as my loss of balance, my baby steps were leaning a little this way, then a little that way then the other way again, and so on many, many times until I found the leaning that worked for me.

Even such small strides, which at the time I believed to be very scary and risky, increased my Zone of Comfort.

Putting passion in one's life often has the ingredient of risk. If it is *reasonable* risk then it falls under the ambience of the Zone of Comfort.

Reasonable risks are in my comfort zone when I move to a place where I am ready for the consequences of that risk. Baby steps increase the size of your Zone of Comfort and minimize the consequences of the risk being taken. Increasing the Zone of Comfort may be the baby steps I took to get there - small strides to boost my courage enough to risk.

Consider a situation many people have experienced, peering over a cliff. For some it is not a reasonable risk to do this without a security system and even then some people inch over to the edge of the cliff to look over and down. Some people do this without precaution and may see any precaution as ridiculous. The Zone of Comfort for the first group of people, the riskier group, is much larger than the precautionary people because the first group may seem to have more courage as they took reasonable risks previously to increase their Zone of Comfort.

Some consequences can be surprising even if it is within the Zone of Comfort. Was being a passenger in a ride-along in a police car a reasonable risk? I thought so at the time, but it had consequences not to be imagined. Nonetheless, it is important and crucial to expand the Zone of Comfort to move through life in a forward motion. Otherwise our fear stops us from progressing through life and we become stagnant.

In my career as a personal and organizational consultant, and teacher, public speaking is a foundation. Speaking in public was scary for me before I got into that kind of business. I took small steps to increase my courage to do public speaking. When I returned to work after my trauma, I was totally determined to return and totally scared. My mouth wasn't working the way it used to. My brain wasn't working the way it used to. My body wasn't working the way it used to!

I didn't realize what a great risk I was taking when I returned to work. I was overreaching and left my Zone of Comfort. I was stubborn and driven so I returned to work in little time bits (half hour a day) coupled with little work bits - easy work, like seeing my office and becoming familiarized with it again, with my vocational therapist present.

Increasing our Zone of Comfort by taking reasonable risks with baby steps facilitates the operation of the other strategies. And this enables us to put passion in our lives.

Once again, to increase my Zone of Comfort was my *choice*. The first step in using all these Iceberg Strategies is the step of choice. My determination supported my choice to increase my Zone of Comfort and to try to return to the work I did before, based in public speaking. Whatever steps I took to increase my Zone of Comfort, I felt the fear and did it anyway!

The Venting Valve
And
The 80/20 Rule

I enter my Zone of Comfort and I change my thinking and language to live my life. Still my complaining floats to the surface of my Iceberg – sometimes it shoots to the surface with a bullet. This is when I use my Venting Valve.

I'm human. I get overwhelmed. I complain. The Venting Valve is a strategy I developed to maintain my attitude and positive forward motion. I follow the 80/20 Rule.

The 80/20 Rule gives us permission to feel and think almost anything. We have to feel the highs and the lows. The Rule invites us to welcome venting, complaining, feeling blue and so forth but only up to 20% of our time, daily, weekly, monthly, yearly, and then to devote 80% of our time to solutions, considering what works, thriving, being optimistic, and so forth. This helps us move forward rather than being stagnant or going backward, without being deliberate.

When I want to vent, complain, feel sorry for myself, or be depressed I allow myself to do that following the 80/20 Rule. I allow myself 20 percent time or less to vent. I know that spending more time at venting or feeling depressed is putting myself deeper in the muck and mire of the pound-of-dirt. It helps me know low to more appreciate the high.

One time I was invited out to a marriage celebration - a stag and doe. When the time came to get ready, I was feeling blue – what was that all about? I didn't know. Besides it was a waste of energy at the time to ponder the reason I was blue. I just was and that was all there was to it. Having no impact on anyone else since I didn't have a date, I decided to stay home by myself and be depressed. I wanted and needed to be depressed. It's normal for people to be depressed, now and then. I decided staying home by myself would be my 20 percent of feeling blue.

I knew that when the next day dawned I would move into my 80 percent of going forward – either through a natural process from a night's sleep or by me making it happen by using some or all of these Strategies.

In the Venting Valve, for example, we complain up to 20% of the time while the remaining 80% of the time we look for solutions. Searching for solutions, we discover what's right with the situation. We look for the opportunities that are present; the opportunities may be hard to see but they are always present, even in difficult times. It may be necessary to magnify the opportunities present to make them a bigger part of our lives. (The Chinese recognize this duality hence the healthy attitude and action that moves forward through the danger.)

It may look and feel counterintuitive to be in your 20 percent. But that moves you forward, as well. It's like eating junk food once a week when you are on a heath kick. We all need to blow off steam and complain. It's human instinct to vent. Fundamentally, venting or complaining is for self-protection. However, it can also get things accomplished – we learn from what we live. It starts in our youth. We see others complain and it gets them what they want. We learn to follow suit. Complaining is the order of the day. People making the decisions allow complaining to work and, therefore, complaining is rewarded. The squeaky wheel gets the grease. However, complaining is often hurtful and child-like and can create dysfunction now or later.

Unless it's understood as using your Venting Valve, bad complaining creates stagnation and an unhealthy attitude. Venting as part of your 'good' complaining to be heard in a helpful and constructive manner creates forward motion and identifies or poses solutions.

PRLs of Wisdom*

St. Bernard of Clairvanxcaid:

"Nothing can work the damage except myself I am a real sufferer by my fault."

THE MAGNIFICATION

When people are given a compliment, they often brush it away and minimize it. 'Very attractive sweater', some would say. 'Oh, this old thing - just yanked from the bottom of my dresser', might be a response. When events or successes, especially small ones, occur in life they are often either ignored, seen as anomalies, or they are minimized, for example, 'Last Tuesday went well but the rest of the week was awful, as usual'.

Like most people, I struggled with compliments in my past.

I would minimize the complement or task and turn it into a small part of my life. I might even make it so small it would disappear. That did nothing for my accomplishments, nothing for me, and minimized the other person giving me the compliment.

When I do something well I tend to pat myself on the back. Or when something is not useful I focus on the learning I can gain from the experience.

I enlarge what I did well or magnify something about my task that served me well. This magnification makes it a greater part of my life which leads to more gratifying results from accomplished tasks. Success breeds success. So magnifying small successes gives them a greater profile in my life and I pay more attention to them. They are no longer anomalies. Big or small a success is a success! Now when someone compliments me I simply say 'thank you'.

Saying 'Thank you' gets into the dynamics of the Strategies. I only usually look at what worked rather than what didn't work. I look at what didn't work when it moves me forward. If what didn't work must first be rectified before anything else will move me forward, then I pay attention to that. Then I would magnify paying attention to that to make that into a compliment. So rather than focus on what didn't work I magnify and compliment my learning. Now I know what doesn't work! This is always a win-learn situation! It is either a solution that worked or it's learning. There is no failure only feedback. I win all the time because nothing is a loss!

An example is the wheelchair again – it does seem to be a good example. Part of what kept me from not walking, and there were a few reasons, was my balance. In my wheelchair I had to lean this way or that way to find the right balance. I magnify the smallest thing to enable me to see it better in my mind's eye. It may have only been a few centimetres to get it right. I would lean this way. No, that didn't work. I would lean a few centimetres in the same direction. No, that didn't work. And so it went, I tried a thousand leanings and directions to get it right. After each attempt I tried and tried again something different.

Magnify successes, each success! When successes are magnified they grow into large accomplishments. Life is then filled with success, which breeds more success. When you make your successes a bigger part of your life by magnifying them, they crowd out those other times. When your life is filled with successes it, too, works in a synergistic manner. Here again is the synergy of the Iceberg Strategies. Link the magnification of success with choices and attitude. My self-efficacy increases and my attitude grows healthier.

Successes enable us to create more choices in life, which helps confirm self-control leading to more self-power. In organizations, from the roots to the branches within and between all levels - give support, take support - give support, take support.

Magnification of your success does not mean to ignore challenges. In fact, as indicated at the beginning of this book, knowing 'low' is crucial to knowing 'high'. As well, we need to know challenges to know successes.

Again, the strategies are synergistic. In the Venting Valve, I restrict myself to being depressed up to 20 percent of my time. This enables me to really appreciate and know the good times more so! This is not to say "Come on depression, hit me!" but recognizes it as normal.

A word of caution - Newfound successes, strength and information may lead to arrogance and conceit. Then something else has occurred rather than growth like stagnation, destruction or hurt. This is detrimental to you and to your organization – it creates de-synergy.

With your choices and appropriate responsibility you have created true growth in your life. Your positive attitude can grow without swelling your head.

Only 'out-of-control' people have the need to swell their head. They move to arrogance to push people around to increase their strength. This is a false and a short-term way of perceiving and showing power.

The arrogance and pushing others around minimize people's self-power. It is acting out to falsely build power – self-power is sabotaged. These people are, actually, hiding behind a boulder. These people have yet to Explore the Iceberg.

People like this take away the synergy that you are creating with your legitimate self-power in your organization. People like this create the poison at the water cooler (see Appendix IV). Again, you and your organization are on the same page and prefer legitimate self-power rather than false, arrogant, push-around power!

We have often been taught to focus on failures or what went wrong or what doesn't work. Perhaps there was much ridicule from elders growing, or it's the government, or the wrong side of the bed, or the morning coffee. Now is the time to change *what* you look at and *how* you look.

Now that you are approaching the end of the book it is the beginning of the rest of your life. That may sound corny but it's true. I had to start my life over again when I was 45 years old. Perhaps I start my life over every day for each day is the beginning of my life.

Now is the time for no one to push you around and tell you what to do. It's your choice. The question is do you want to create the best profession and organization or do you allow the best to occur elsewhere by not taking action?

Now is the time to put into play all the Iceberg Strategies to create your own personal, professional and organizational growth.

A cousin to the magnification is focusing on solutions. Once again the Venting Valve is in play. Spend no more than twenty percent of your time on what's wrong and, at least, 80% of your time on what works. Magnify what is right and focus on that.

Remember, Babe Ruth struck out more times than he hit home runs. Thomas Edison had a thousand attempts before inventing the light bulb. Edison considered he took almost a thousand steps to invent the light bulb rather than almost a thousand failures. Where would we be today if after his failures he gave up? It could be said we'd be in the dark!

Thomas Edison knew that the only sign of failure is giving up.

Four

The Surface

Thinking and Language

What we think about, we act out. The thinking we use strongly influences how we behave. Therefore, this is another foundational Iceberg Strategy I use.

One strong influence on increasing the Zone of Comfort is how I think and how you think. Starting back to work my fear was dealt with by thinking about the future - The short-term pain for long term gain stuff.

Thinking - Acting

What we think about we act out. Whatever we think drives our actions. Maybe not today, maybe not tomorrow, but someday you will act out what you think.

When you think unhealthy thoughts and you don't change your mind to healthier thoughts then unpleasant things will come out — somehow. Either by what you say or by what you do, it will fester inside and perhaps affect your health.

What I say or the way I think can determine what I want to do. The first important thing I do is to consider what I *want* to have happen as opposed to what I don't want; what I *want* to see rather than what I don't want to see; what *needs* to happen rather than what doesn't need to happen.

For example, don't think of your breathing. Do not think of your breathing. OK, even though you were instructed not to think of your breathing, I can almost guarantee that you suddenly became very conscious of your breathing.

Thinking about what we don't want can prevent us from moving to what we do want. Considering what we don't want can be linked to the "what if" syndrome. Often the "what if" syndrome is used as a rationalization for not acting. To put a twist on a well-known song, "this is the great pretender"! It seems to provide legitimate excuses for not moving forward. At times, it can actually be the great impeder!

Thoughts of what we don't want to happen can overwhelm what we want to have happen because what we think about we act out. Therefore, we can act out what we don't want to have happen.

My example is, again, learning how to walk. When I thought about falling down those thoughts overwhelmed my thoughts of walking. Dwelling on the 'falling down' thoughts impeded my learning how to walk again.

SOLUTIONS

In the beginning of focusing on solutions rather than problems, focusing on what worked rather than what didn't work; focusing on what I wanted rather than what I didn't want; it all seemed contrary. I learned from all other people growing up and in my studies to think about problems. I considered problems that needed to be fixed and in considering problems directed myself to what I didn't want rather than what I wanted. This kept me stuck in the muck and the mire, my pound-of-dirt. In fact, I found myself sinking deeper and deeper in it.

When I changed my language, it changed my thinking. I changed the notion of "problems" to the notion of "barriers". Rather than being stopped by a bog of problems, barriers were a challenge. In fact, I changed the notion of "barriers" to the notion of "challenges" and use it today. Challenges make life fun. Challenges put spice and passion in my life.

I went from being stopped by problems to being challenged by barriers, then to having passion over-flowing with challenges.

In my experience, I have seen no forward motion when individuals and organizations discuss only problems. People tend to go nowhere in the discussion and in practice.

Now, I may identify a problem and define it, then move to the challenges, then go to solutions considering what works.

This kind of language keeps me less overwhelmed in my recovery. I don't consider my recovery wrought with problems. Recovery from a severe incapacitating injury was far from a bowl full of jellybeans. However, rather than considering what I didn't want, I thought of what I wanted, focusing on solutions, which kept me moving forward.

Now, I take full responsibility for creating my solutions. The cliché is 'if it's gonna be, it's up to me'. I need to be clear. I often cannot do it on my own. I am not sufficient unto myself. I give credit where credit is due and allow myself to be corrected when I fail to show appreciation. For example, family, friends, and health care workers were more than supporting me. However, I, and I alone, needed to decide and chose to work and recover or I'd still be rolling in a wheelchair.

LANGUAGE

In waking life, we speak to ourselves at 400 words a minute.

What do you say to yourself? Do you empower yourself with genuinely optimistic words? What do you think about? Do you consider what is wrong with your situation or do you consider what is right?

Change your thinking and change your language.

Put presuppositional words on your statements or questions. Rather than "It hasn't happened", say "It hasn't happened YET". The word 'yet' presupposes it will happen, sometime.

Put an optimistic spin on phrases. Rather than "This doesn't work", ask "What works?" This redirects your thinking from focusing on what didn't happen to magnify what could happen.

Change words to those that expect results. Rather than, "Why can't I invent the light bulb", say "When I invent the light bulb...".

Put words in the form of solutions. Change "why" to "what" or "when" or "how" or "where". Often in our words and tone there is a feeling of guilt or blame held within what and how it is said. Rather than "Why did you do that?" change it to "What prompted you to do that?" or "How come you did that?" Rather than "Why Me?" try "What can I do with this challenge?", "How is it that this happened?' "How will this help me or others?", "What can I do to make this work?"

"Accept challenges, so that you may feel the exhilaration of victory."
-- General George S. Patton

What would happen if Thomas Edison said to himself 'there is no way such a thing as a light bulb will work'? Rather than, 'this won't work', ask, 'what can I do to make this work?', rather than 'problems galore!', say, 'my life is filled with challenges. 'I am eating and digesting my pound-of-dirt.'

Change 'But' to 'And'...

> When the word 'but' is heard it negates the first part of your statement. The word 'and' connects the parts of the statement.
>
> Following a complement we often use the word 'but'. As in the case where we complement by saying – 'Thank you for cleaning your room, <u>but</u> this corner is still messy and needs cleaning.' By using the word 'but', the words following the 'but' undermine the initial complement. It's a difference that can make a difference. Next time, you are invited to use the word 'and'.

Rather than suffering, search for delight.

I am present from beginning to the end. Perhaps I am finding and using the resources needed. I base a lot on cognitive behavioural theory, the Iceberg Strategy of Thinking and Language, to respect my self and others. I tend to turn my thinking around. If I am not trustworthy how can I be trusting? If I am not respecting others how can I respect myself? Respect and love walk hand in hand. If I don't respect and love myself first how can I show it to others?

When I was planting these strategic seeds, I had no idea that I would be using them to recover from a traumatic event in my life! It's imperative to create a future and it is as imperative to handle the unknown. What thoughts do you nurture to rise above anything that comes your way? There are at least two parallel tracks in life. We live for today and plan for tomorrow.

Why Not 'Why?'

The word 'why' often creates guilt and this is energy used unwisely. For example, 'why did I do that?' influences my thinking that I was wrong or too stupid to do something different.

I have largely removed the word 'why' from my vocabulary. I use it infrequently, and then only in social situations. This avoids any 'poor me' syndrome or guilt. In order to think and talk in solutions the word 'why' often gets in the way and becomes a problem. It also dwells on what happened and sometimes knowing what happened is a time waster. Is it really important to know what happened to me? Will knowing what happened make my recovery easier? It's an interesting story but is not needed in my recovery. I'd do the same things; work as hard; and be as frustrated.

PRLs of Wisdom*

John Milton said,

"The mind is its own place and in itself can make a Heaven of Hell and a Hell of Heaven"

In the wheel chair I usually did not wonder 'why did this happen to me?' That was energy that got me nowhere. I needed to put my energy into strategies that moved me forward.

Where are the Where's, the When's, the What's and How's?

Rather than 'why', I start questions that culminate in forward motion. The words - 'what', 'when', 'where', 'how' -- are wise. They start and end with useful energy. Questions that begin with these words usually focus on behaviours and often end with synergistic solutions.

Rather than say, "Why did I do that?" I say, "What can I do differently?" or "What can I do to make this happen?"

Using the other behavioural or solution words might be "When can this happen?", "How can I make this happen?", Where can I make this happen?"

To emphasize, the way we think can influence our language and can impact our behaviour.

Rather than "never forget", use "always remember". Sometimes when we are speaking to someone we say,

"I forgot to tell you ...", say "As I remember, I want to tell you ...".

Rather than, "I made a mistake", use "I'll do it differently next time".

Rather than saying what you don't want, say what you *do* want. For example, when instructing your children instead of saying – 'Don't play on the road' say 'Play in the park'.

When I take full responsibility for things happening in my life it helps met avoid the 'blame game'. The 'blame game' is useless energy that takes away my control of solutions.

Maybe walking again was to be out of my control. Perhaps my perseverance, effort and patience would not be enough to make me walk again. So I would learn from the process rather than the result. It's the journey not the destination.

In themselves, individual words may be seen as small pieces of life yet they are a difference that can make a difference. A change in thinking and language are giant steps toward a goal. If your goal, like winning a lottery, is based more on chance than on your own action, your change in thinking and language will not increase your chances of successfully winning the lottery (although there is a little voice that would say it does – I'm not there yet – although, it can't hurt).

Change my language to fit my situation. With regards to the future, rather than say "Wait and see", I turn it around and say,

"act and create!"

Destiny is not passive. Destiny is active. Rather than wait for destiny to happen I take action to create it, within the boundaries set by the universe, rather than lose total control of my life. This is a time to create strength and wisdom.

PRLs of Wisdom*

*We choose for our thoughts to be the
chain around an elephant's leg...
or ...the wings of an eagle...*

Black and White Thinking

As described earlier, Black and White Thinking was one of my downfalls. Black and White Thinking kept me stuck in the muck and the mire of the pound-of-dirt. I was making my pound-of-dirt deeper or thicker by my extreme thoughts.

Now I've turned the notion of Black and White Thinking around and use it to my advantage. Rather than making it a deficit of mine I use it as strength.

When I hear myself using that kind of deficit language it is a cue to me that I am overwhelmed by something. Maybe I already know I'm overwhelmed and my Black and White language confirms it. Maybe I don't know yet that I'm overwhelmed and this language tells me that I should pay more attention to what is overwhelming me and take action.

The word 'never' is an example of Black and White Thinking. I will *never* get better. Is Black and White Thinking telling me I'm stressed? No. It's telling me the truth, which might be stressful - sometimes the truth hurts. I will never get better from my trauma. I will never be 100 percent of who and where I was. That word and language is telling me the truth. It tells me that I need to take action to live with my new life, forever - and get used to it!

The following inclusive words are intrinsic in Black and White Thinking. It is important to move to continuum thinking. Put thoughts and actions on a continuum.

Some words I use in my thoughts or out loud follow. Rather than extreme words like 'never' or 'always' the word 'sometimes' indicates a continuum. An example is: "I never get anything right" and notice the difference between "Sometimes I get things right".

Rather than the word 'if', I substitute the more definitive word 'when'. Instead of: "If I succeed" I say "When I succeed".

Rather than the word 'might', I use the word 'will'. An example is: "I might Explore the Iceberg" I say, "I will Explore the Iceberg".

Once again, this brings positive energy for forward motion and entertains passion in your life!

Using the Venting Valve releases built up tension from the over whelming pound-of-dirt.

In most places, especially, in large organizations, venting upwards is blocked or people think that it is blocked. This perceived blocking often occurs through poor communication, a trust issue, or the 'blame game' (at times, a political move to encourage mythical awareness of those above).

The Venting Valve is used at water coolers. To use the necessary venting valve, staff vent laterally, toward each other, either by complaining, getting angry about each other, being disrespectful and so forth.

Often venting and complaining is self-protection, for example, it's the other person or thing that's the problem - 'it's not my fault'. Also, the individual who is complaining often perceived as having power with a group of staff in the organization. Then this staff group follows the line of complaining and they are often perceived as having power within the organization. All of this occurs because it's easier to complain than find solutions and projects the fault onto another person or thing.

The perceived blocking can lead to self-protection which can be unhealthy for the group or dangerous – for you, for your group, and for your organization. Venting is contagious and tends not to result in action to resolve the issue. In fact, in venting there is no action. Simply hot air. When the Venting Valve operates under the 80/20 Rule, the staff and organization follow the line upwards toward synergy. Venting is healthier when it has time boundaries of no more than 20 percent.

P.E.P. Talk

Give yourself a PEP Talk.

As I described earlier I was physically fit at the time of the accident. Notwithstanding the spiritual benefit of my meditating/praying everyday, this activity also enhanced my physical and mental fitness - synergistic. This broadened my foundation for living.

After the trauma I was unable to do one push up standing facing the wall. Anything I attempted was very painful.

I put trust into a health care institution and staff that I didn't even know. It is counterintuitive to put intimate trust into people you've never met. It is definitely 'lovers and other strangers' scenario. That's what health care is about.

The new me couldn't run anymore, I was in a wheelchair. The clear thinking was gone and I couldn't think straight. I couldn't remember things or people. I was no longer the self-sufficient man. In my mind, I was less than a man. My middle names were 'trials' and 'tribulation'.

Most activity hurt and was very limited. The physiotherapy confirmed to me that I useless and weak. In the beginning it was discouraging and painful and hard to see results through the trauma.

I had to start again. My physical fitness and strength was wiped out. My brain was wiped out. My relationship was wiped out. Paul was wiped out.

I kept talking to myself. Although outwardly, my articulation had taken a beating, I could, at least, be articulate internally – and to this day I wonder about that ability. I talked to myself everyday. With the hospital staff being so encouraging in their remarks, I copied them with my self-talk.

Long ago I planted a seed in me to nurture compliments and encouragers from others and from myself. So, rather than minimize the optimistic advice and words the hospital staff gave, I enhanced their words as I spoke to me. I have called this **P.E.P. Talk** and turned the word PEP into an acronym. These are qualities and values I needed and we all need to get through our challenges. They are:

Perseverance

Effort

Patience

If we persevere with our effort and have patience, the successful outcome will be yours and mine.

With all that I had to do in my recovery, from physiotherapy to speech therapy and more, I had to persevere with great effort and have patience that I would improve. At that time I wanted to improve RIGHT NOW. Then my patience was slim. Now I know that with appropriate patience things will happen, perhaps not in the time frame I want it to happen but it will happen. As long as I take responsibility for my perseverance and effort, patience will bring me a successful outcome or the outcome that I need.

My story is a great example of P.E.P. Talk. I put perseverance behind my effort and was patient with the results. That is how I worked to get where I am post trauma!

P. erseverance

Perseverance is the operative word that you and I need. Some people then, and especially now, call my perseverance stubbornness. "Do you ever give up!? You're so stubborn", some would say. "Stubborn?" I would say. Perhaps, yet it got me where I wanted to go – stronger, walking, wiser. I Persevered. There is no failure, only feedback. The only mark of failure is giving up.

E. ffort

Effort is the challenge you and I need. When I did physiotherapy and do physiotherapy (these days it's mostly a workout with a hint of physiotherapy in mind) it was hard, painful, discouraging and seemingly slow in its results. Putting P.erseverance behind my E.ffort kept my E.ffort strong.

P. atience

Patience is a must. I made a choice to hold on to my Patience. Having Patience is like watching a newly seeded garden grow. It takes time and nurturing. Plant a flower or seed; it takes time to blossom, not in the time you want - in its own time - its own voice.

If I was not supposed to walk even with giving all my Perseverance, Effort, Patience, then I know, now, that I respect the decision, outside of my control. This is a far distance from Black and White Thinking - 'I'll never walk again.'

Individually or together our vital P.E.P. Talk cannot be sustained 100% of the time. P.E.P. Talk, in reality, is an ebb and flow. I get tired of the work I need to do, or the situation, or of my frustration.

Each of the elements – Perseverance, Effort, Patience – follow the 80/20 Rule of the Venting Valve. While all these are important, they cannot be sustained 100% of the time.

My patience and perseverance, at times, wear thin. But I put these times in the 20% category and lead myself into the other 80% if it is not happening naturally.

For example, exercising. Sometimes I don't want to exercise. I'd rather watch TV. My choice starts with a question to myself. What gets me more of what I want, exercise or TV? How much time do I need for either? Where will I be mentally and emotionally at the end of the activity? What could I be doing instead? What matters most right now, tomorrow, next week, in five year's time?

These questions challenge my thinking a lot of the time. Often I learn from trial and 'feedback' (remember, there is no 'error'). To use the TV/exercising example, one time I watch TV and the next time I exercise. Then I compare and see which one served me best in my mind, body and spirit. The resolve may not be complete but it's the journey that creates passion in my life!

PRLs of Wisdom*

Jean De Le Fontaine said:

Patience and time do more than force and rage.

PRLs of Wisdom*

J.P. Jacks said:

An optimist is one who sees an opportunity in every difficulty. A pessimist is one who sees a difficulty in every opportunity.

PRLs of Wisdom*

Know that pushing a wave to shore any faster than the ocean brings it in, is futile ...

FIVE

THE DEPTHS

BALANCING LIFE

This is what it is all about - Balancing Life!

Balancing Life impeccably is like walking on water. I think of this metaphor because of what has been taught to us for thousands of years by Jesus, Buddha, Mohammed, the mentors of today

The Balancing Life Diagram

We are born. One certainty in life is that we die. And in between life is a pound-of-dirt - because we make it so!

This extreme comment is not contrary to the fact that we all need challenges in our life to grow. Problems do create a pound-of-dirt. Challenges do not. Challenges make life interesting; fill it with passion. A life without passion is a life denied. Let's say life is a pound-of-dirt between living and dying. Is this a foregone conclusion? Do you want to grumble all your life or do you want to create a great life and organization?

In the diagram there is an inverted triangle for a reason. Life is precarious and filled with challenges. It is a balancing act.

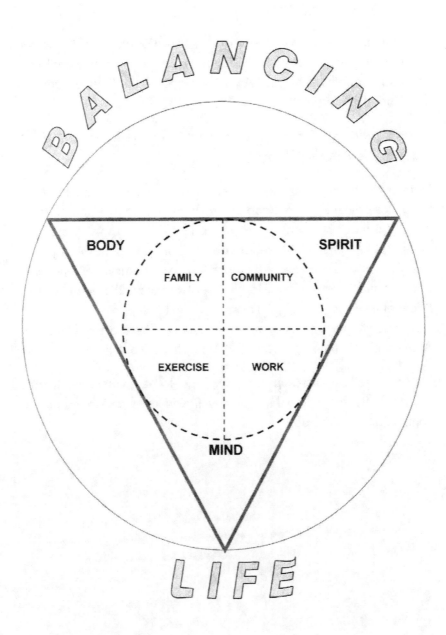

Do we not gain more control in our lives by taking complete responsibility for it? Taking responsibility prevents the 'blame game' or the 'what if' syndrome that strangles us.

As individuals we keep our own life balanced or off kilter. Again, we have to take responsibility for that determination. Do you want to put your life in another's hands? Again, we go into the 'blame game' or the 'what if' syndromes.

These syndromes of blaming and 'what if' can push us around like Black and White Thinking.

In my own situation and experience, where would it get me if I blamed the police officer for what happened? Where would it get me if I asked 'what if it didn't happen; where would I be?' The answer is simple – nowhere! - At least, nowhere forward. The energy spent solving these questions is wasted. These questions truly are the never-ending story because there is no answer to them. I also believe that the injury, as Michael J. Fox says, is a gift. I'm right where I'm supposed to be; living a passionate life with meaning and purpose. There are still times my Acquired Brain Injury pushes me around, but I live with it.

No one is self-sufficient, however, 'If it's got to be it's up to me'. Taking responsibility for where I am in my life in no way abandons my connections and support.

FOUNDATIONAL ELEMENTS AND INGREDIENTS

The Balancing Life Diagram is self-explanatory when all aspects of it are considered. The three apexes (Mind, Body, Spirit) are Foundational Elements. The four quadrants in the internal circle (Family, Community, Work, Exercise) are the Ingredients. All the Elements and Ingredients contained are needed to bake the cake and keep life balanced. Anything healthy and appropriately responsible you add is icing on the cake.

All elements and ingredients are needed. However, the Element and Ingredient measurements will change from person to person. For example, one may do more community work while another does more family time and involvement. The ingredients are measures of time and/or involvement. We all have opinions about what is important – is this more important than that and so on? Measured importance is perceptual and is up to each individual's thinking.

The measures have changed in my life since the trauma. To begin with all my time has been impacted by my fatigue, thinking ability, and my current life patterns. I am involved with all Elements and Ingredients but some to a lesser degree. For example, I still volunteer at my church but not as much time and with less responsibility. Before my injury I chaired an intense committee loaded with responsibilities. Now I am a member of a committee with less time involvement and less onerous decisions.

I coached soccer in the community before my injury. Changes in my life, lifestyle, physical challenges and my fatigue at night have displaced me from that activity.

I am still committed to health in moderation yet I am no longer as involved in my exercise routine. As described, I changed my regime and timing. Instead of the first couple of hours of the morning I do a half hour at lunch and what I can do at other times of the day or week.

This is what is so valuable about balancing life. It is all in each person's control! Sure, there may be judgments and opinions from others about what is important or what holds more value. But it is still in each person's control.

Both the internal circle and the quadrants are hash lines. The intent is to show diagrammatically that in the essence of life they are not separate. The broken lines enable the imperative *flow* between all the Ingredients and the Foundational Elements. Flow creates synergy within us. We become more when all are involved in our lives - even if we only have space in our lives for a little bit of involvement. It is total balance of life when this happens. Our experiences give us our stories to continue Exploring the Iceberg.

The circle of life surrounds the inverted triangle. Take your own meaning of the circle of life but it does indicate we are all connected.

The next few pages consider the three Foundational Elements in the Balancing Life inverted triangle - Mind, Body and Spirit.

THE FOUNDATIONAL ELEMENTS
AND THEIR INGREDIENTS

The Iceberg Strategy of Thinking and Language (from the cognitive-behavioural theory) works like this.

The Foundational Elements exist – like earth, wind and fire. These elements are the habitat for all our experiences.

Experiences happen. Experiences are interpreted by our perceptions. Perceptions are filters that experiences pass through in our mind.

We choose our actions and behaviour from our perceptions or our interpretation of what happened. It's not the event, it's the perception of the event (Albert Einstein)

The results of our actions influence our thinking. Was our action successful? Did we feel good? Of course this is all relative to the individual; our interpretation of success. This starts to look like the map of life rather than the circle of life. The diagram shows that the process is far from linear. Each influences the other but it has to begin with an experience. The following diagram is like an over-simplified spider's web.

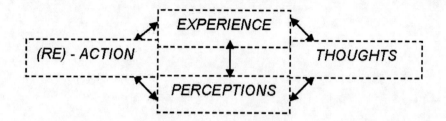

This creates who we are. And who we are comes about from the way we think and our perceptions emanating from our life stories. Nothing is carved in stone this way. It is very pliable and flexible. Any past story, for example, can be reinterpreted any time. This gives us the opportunity to make our life, profession and organization the best by the way we think...

The Feelings Conundrum:

Feelings come about through our perceptions, usually. How we interpret the experience is how we choose the feeling. Feelings, at times, are so overwhelming and swamp our thoughts, that it's difficult to understand which came first.

My belief is that as an infant we are driven by our feelings. We cannot reason, think or understand the world around us so we 'feel' the world. As our mind matures with age, giving us experiences and learning, we begin to form thoughts. These thoughts come to the fore. We may then minimize our feelings to keep our thoughts in control of the world.

Our feelings are deep within us. However, we are often afraid of them and what they could bring - the unknown and, inherently, our inability to control them. Therefore our thoughts come to power to maintain a sense of control and order.

THE FOUNDATIONAL ELEMENTS – THE HABITAT OF EXPERIENCES

Body

Is exercising your preferred activity? After exercising do you think differently? Is your mind clearer and energized by the endorphins flowing through your body?

I exercised. I ate healthily. What can I say except my physical fitness was a strong determinant in my survival. My physical condition was like the buttress around a fortress. I can't prove it for myself. I feel strongly that it kept me going physically. My heart simply kept on pumping through its strength and wisdom!!

There is a plethora of literature about a healthy lifestyle. You will find your own approach to maintain your body through food management and exercise.

Spirit

Spirit is the power within us that gives us courage and stamina to face and live with the truths in our lives.

Belief in yourself and a higher power – one is better, both are best. I manifest my spirituality in Christianity. You may manifest it differently. Spirituality is crucial.

There is much in life that is out of our control. Faith enlarges our Zone of Comfort to enable us to balance life better. To the extent that I have recovered, I thank my Higher Power, God. Will I recover even more? I don't know. Did I know I would recover as much as I have? Did I know I would walk again?

I did know that whatever happened, my faith would stabilize me. I had faith that the conclusion would be what needed to happen for me to contribute to my life and to the lives of others. Whatever happened to me, it would be for the best. My faith helped me believe that. I needed that because I didn't know my future.

Faith enables one to welcome the future.

Giving up was not in the equation. My faith did not alleviate the work I had to do. I still had to do the vast amount of work necessary to get what I wanted. Faith helped me understand that if my work did not provide me with what I wanted then *life* was telling me what I *needed* -for me to do something with what I was given.

When I walk across the street, I still look both ways before crossing. Faith won't stop me from getting hit by any traffic.

Belief in a higher power enables me to know there *is* a gift in the cards I'm dealt. Belief in myself enables me to know I can see and have the power to use it to my advantage or beyond me.

Faith in a Higher Power can open me up to everything in my control and, especially, out of my control. It enhances the belief in myself and know what I believe I can do and my limits. I can feel the fear and do it anyway knowing that I am viewing the unknown from a higher perspective.

Mind

Balancing Life is like an inverted triangle, with the Foundational Element of 'mind' in the lower apex. You can keep the triangle balanced or set it off kilter depending on your perceptions, which you create through your thinking.

Our perception can create our attitude. Our attitude is primary to how we live with our life, our family, our profession, and our organization.

Using the Iceberg Strategies moves us forward to perceptions that work to our advantage. The 'why me' and 'blame game' syndromes creep in and influence perceptions. These syndromes *creep in* because they're as creepy as a Stephen King story.

I said I complain and feel sorry for myself, however, no more than 20 percent of the time. I complain about what happens to me. There are times when I think – 'I can't believe this happened!' I had many plans in place before the trauma and injury happened but my life is different. What can I do now?

Sometimes I get so tired and frustrated I want to give up and simply slouch from exhaustion. There are times I don't care. When I hear myself think that way I put the challenge aside and simply rest. Sometimes I want a soft shoulder to be there and there isn't one. So I buck up and rely on my P.atience in P.E. P. Talk!

If I perceived the injury to be the end of my life, where would I be? I perceive the trauma and injury as an occurrence that had to happen *for* me and *for* many people in my life and those who are yet to be a part of my life. My experiences since the trauma happened have confirmed my thoughts. My mind is giving me a win-learn situation and it creates a synergistic life, profession and organization.

I talk about the trauma happening 'for' me and rather than 'to' me. This is an example of the Strategy of Thinking and Language. One small word in thinking and verbalizing is a difference that can make a difference.

Attitude is what we own. No one can take away our thinking or attitude, no matter our circumstances. Our mind is the playground for our Attitude.

Attitude – It's our choice

PRLs of Wisdom*

Choice happens with <u>you</u> or without <u>you</u>...

Attitude/Choice

Choice happens with us or without us. We make the choice or the choice is made for us - by someone else, or the fact that not making a choice is making a choice. Do we like power being taken away from us? Do we like being out of control? That is what can happen when other people make decisions that affect us.

Having no choice takes away our self-power by taking away our involvement in any decisions that impact our lives. At the very least, when choice exists and we *do not* make a decision, we *have* made a decision.

Giving ourselves no choice also takes away our responsibility for ourselves, which gives away our power and control over ourselves. Again, these notions are inter linked like a spider's web.

As most parents know, bedtime for their children may not be a simple task. Not only the children may feel they want to do something else, deep down inside them is the notion of being pushed around. To alleviate the situation, give them a choice, not whether to go to bed or not to go to bed. Give them choice around, for example, timing, where to go to bed, or perhaps to go to the easy way or the hard way! It's their choice and decision, and that choice gives them power over the situation, and they are learning to make decisions for themselves and take responsibility.

It's a beautiful thing. Again the spider's web analogy comes to mind. The effect of these small behaviours in each home can link to other small behaviours in upbringing that accumulate to make the world an even better place! Far-fetched? - I think not.

I lost feeling like a grown man. Choices were taken away and I didn't ask for that to happen. It's hard to appreciate the help when people look after you as if you are a child and I was child that came from being an independent adult. After the trauma I was the child from the man!

Choice is also powerful and empowering. It empowers children and also staff in organizations. Bring people on board with the decisions so that they have a part of the decisions that impact on them. A basic part of child rearing is teaching youngsters how to make valuable decisions and choices. This increases self-efficacy. It injects empowerment into the youngsters until they understand the concept behaviourally and are cognitively mature to empower themselves. The same basic thinking holds true for staff of an organization. As much as possible bring staff in on decisions that affect them. Move them through a process to make that happen. Staff becomes involved in the decision that impacts on them - even when others make the final decision. Being involved is opposite to being ignored and no one wants to be ignored. Being ignored is tantamount to the greatest fear next to death - ostracism.

Because choice is very powerful then the more choices we have, the more control we have of ourselves. It is imperative to create as many choices as possible for each of us - the more choices the better decisions.

In any situation I increase my choices rather than wait for someone else to do that for me. I keep myself in control of my life. There may seem to be no choices. Actually, there are always more choices, even simply one more!

Turning Points and Choice Points

As I mentioned earlier my marriage ended. This was a *turning* point in my life. Following the *turning* point it was up to me to create *choice* points. At the time I gave myself two choices – live or die. I wanted to choose to die. Obviously, I didn't die. Black and White Thinking was pushing me around. It was telling me that suicide was the easiest solution with the least amount of work and best decisions for everyone, especially me.

The psychiatrist wanted to commit me. My next *choice* point was to be committed or change my mind from being suicidal. Changing my mind meant creating behaviour other than suicide. I thought about the values my parents raised me with; I thought about how my siblings supported me; I thought about my children and the meaning of their lives in mine. Did I want to be the ultimate disappointment by killing myself? Or did I want to take on the supportive and compassionate behaviour I was being shown without soliciting it? This latter side of the 'question coin' is a core value of mine – to be valuable. Everyone wants to have value. Having value - a core for us all. What drew me away from suicide or the dark side of Black and White Thinking was choosing to remember the supportive compassion of my family.

I chose to change my mind.

This accumulative and ultimate *choice* point became a *turning* point in my life, thanks to my family. I wanted and needed to become worthwhile and valuable. Rather than plant the question 'why did I do that?" I planted the seed to grow by asking myself 'what can I do now?' and 'how will I become valuable?'

I asked these questions of myself years ago. There have been many answers. This book is one of them.

Some questions to consider when creating choices are as follows:

- Have I considered and understood the situation correctly?

- Have I changed my language or my thoughts – my perceptions – to adapt the existing choices?

- Have I considered the situation differently, focused on what works or is valuable in the situation?

- Have I gone beyond myself and considered how others or the community can use my situation to their benefit? Sometimes it's not all about me.

The times when no choices seem available, I bring out my metaphorical magnifying glass and enlarge the circumstance to enlarge any other choices available. For example, I focus on my language. I notice what can be changed. Language use is a difference that can make a difference. Do I want to be the best *in* the world, or the best *for* the world?

Choice

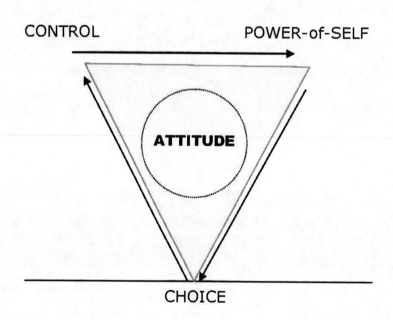

To summarize the diagram about Attitude it shows choice is foundational to Attitude. There is always a choice. The only time choice is taken away is when there is a loaded gun held by someone at our temples (some would say that even then there is choice).

The more choices we have the more control we exert in our lives. The more control we have the stronger we feel –leads to more personal power.

This power is not to be confused with power to push people around. That is something other than power. The power is internal to have control in your life.

Choice gives us responsibility for our thinking and actions and, therefore, empowers us. Empowerment helps create self-control.

Choice leads to control that leads to self-power and that leads back to choice. Choice gets stronger making control stronger making self-power stronger and back to choice. Choice leads to control leading to power-of-self leading back to choice. This enables us to create more choices which gives us more control and more self-power. And so it goes, the synergy is there again – more than the sum of its parts.

Sometimes, I have gone into Black and White Thinking, especially when I'm feeling overwhelmed or tired. There are several choices I have available. I can give up, or put things on the back burner for later consumption, or I can sit quietly and rely on my stillness to know, or I can exercise, or I can watch television. Rather than throw the baby out with the bath water, I put aside my book for a short time and stop. I am so tired, I need rest.

What we look at in life is negligible as to *how* we look at life. It is not the event; it is the perception of the event.

Being empowered and in control of our situation aligns the notion of power with self-efficacy. Self-efficacy is the belief in ourselves that we can be accomplished. Others can believe we can accomplish something. But usually, it is not until our self-efficacy tells us that we can do it, we have the confidence to just do it. Often outside supports and belief help us gain that self-efficacy. We need to believe in ourselves.

Now that's attitude that won't quit – your own belief in you! Be your own inspiration!!

Further, if the accomplishment is not being actualized, our attitude finds accomplishment in the process. Our attitude can use this accomplishment for other experiences. The accomplishment is the journey not the destination. It is learning and the journey can take that learning to the next level.

Choice is a change agent and is foundational because it depends on us. It depends on how or what we think about our situations or experiences.

Our attitude is built from the ground up like families and organizations, from our choices. Before, I used the spider web analogy. Spiders sit in the middle of their web. Our thoughts sit in the middle of our web and the flow begins – the synergy of which I speak highly - choice, self-control, self-power creating our core – our attitude.

There is no better way to live and be.

ATTITUDE

Charles Swindol

The longer I live, the more I realize the impact of attitude
on life.
Attitude, to me is more important than facts.
It is more important than the past, than education, than money,
than what other people think or say or do.
It is more important than appearance, giftedness, or skill.
It will make or break a company ... a church ... a home.
The remarkable thing is we have choice every day regarding
the attitude we will embrace in a certain way.
We cannot change the inevitable.
The only thing we can do is play on the one
string we have, and that is our attitude.

LIFE IS 10% WHAT HAPPENS TO ME
AND 90% HOW I REACT TO IT.

And so it is with you ... we are in charge of our attitudes.

Charles Swindol

http://home.xnet.com/~ansible/attitude.html
http://faculty.kutztown.edu/friehauf/attitude.html

PRLs of Wisdom*

The Bible says in Rom. 12: 4-8:

"For as we have many members in one body, and all members have not the same office: So we, being many, are one body... and every one members of another.

*Having then gifts differing..."
(*Noted by Myers and Briggs)

Jungian Personalities
Through Myers-Briggs Type Indicator
(MBTI)

What Is Type?

This Iceberg Strategy explores the deepest part of the Iceberg for you to strive to thrive.

The following will provide some information about the work of Carl Gustav Jung and Isabel Myers and Katharine C. Briggs (more can be accessed in Appendices I, II & III). Chapter 11 outlines a process for learning your type and Chapter 12 provides thumbnail descriptions of all 16 types provided by Dr. C. George Boeree.

Swiss psychiatrist Carl Gustav Jung has been highly regarded for his work during and after his time with Sigmund Freud.

Jung was born in 1875 and lived until 1961. He is associated with and developed the Stages of Life, the Phenomenology of Self, and what is discussed here- Psychological Types, 1921.

Psychological type is an explanation of human personality. Myers and Briggs made Jung's complex wok more easily accessible to the general population by placing it into language understood by all. Based on Jung's foundational work on Personality Types, Myers and Briggs developed the most widely use assessment of today - the Myers-Briggs Type Indicator (MBTI, 1942). MBTI, and Myers-Briggs type Indicator are registered trademarks of the Myers-Briggs Type Indicator in the United States and other countries.

There are many different personality questionnaires or assessments that have been developed. The Myers-Briggs Type Indicator is the foundation to most personality assessments. The MBTI assessment helps define your personality type, confirm what you know about yourself, and discovers new information about yourself. Find a qualified or certified administrator/counsellor through a learning centre, Association of Psychological Type (CAPT Canada), information on the Internet, or through me (www.paullamb.ca).

People, with whom we interact, reason differently than we do. They value different things. Our interests are different than others'.

We are complex. Hence, no one thing or expert can explain all human behaviour. However, the four areas considered by Jung, and Myers and Briggs describe four fundamental preferences for life:

- From where we get our energy

- To what we pay attention

- How we make decisions

- How we act in life

These four preferences provide us with a 4-letter description of personality type. For example, I am an INFJ personality type. The letters will be defined and described in the following chapter.

Six

The Self-Choice Assessment

This chapter will lead you to discover your Myers-Briggs Type Indicator (MBTI) through completing a simple self-assessment. It is a fun process and I encourage you to complete it before continuing your read.

It is imperative to recognize that all types are good. The world is made up of all 16 types. The MBTI sorts rather than measures. The self-score attached to each preference is not an indication of how good or poor you are in that preference, but describes your strength of preference, only. The number you calculate from the following charts is your self-scored number which may be different from an MBTI assessment you have completed or will complete in the future. Your score and determination of your type through this process will be useful.

The following charts and descriptions are aligned with the four dichotomies of preferences described by Jung, and Myers and Briggs.

In the following charts, the preferences are described generically as Preference One to Four. This is to avoid any bias that you may associate with social and cultural definitions of the words used to describe the four preferences.

Each chart describes dichotomous poles on a continuum.

This is intentionally a forced choice dichotomy with no 'in-between'. After completing the 4 charts, you will have 8 letters (4 pairs) that will be connected to 8 numbers.

Directions for the Self-Score Process:

1. In the two lists within each chart, read the paired descriptions. They are opposite in meaning. Choose only one, by checking one bullet point. Rather than linger, record your reaction after reading them one after the other. If you just can't decide, then it is better to go with your initial reaction. Which one struck you first?

A hypothetical example from Chris is provided below:

☐   I prefer the colour red

☒   I prefer the colour blue

In the above example, Chris may like and use each colour but prefers the colour 'blue' and so chose that one.

2. When you have completed the chart, add the checks up and total them at the bottom of each respective chart. The column with the highest number will describe you chosen preference.

3. Keep this information available to refer to later and read on.

Each Preference is prefaced with a story. In which character do you mostly see yourself?

PREFERENCE ONE
THE PARTY

*B*ill goes to a party. When Bill enters the party he does a reconnaissance to identify people he knows. Once recognizing friends, Bill goes to the kitchen and pours a drink and pauses in the kitchen by sipping the drink so it looks to the others (and perhaps, to himself) to have a legitimate reason to delay before joining the party. In fact, Bill already thinks that he has joined the party. Bill is simply getting a drink. In actuality, he is building energy to enjoy the party to its fullest. Going out where the guests are gathered he approaches his friends. Through introductions by his friends he meets other people.

When Sally enters the party she says, exuberantly 'OK, everyone, let the party begin, now that I'm here'. Then she says: 'I'll have a rum and coke, no ice'. Then, Sally, to start the party (for it starts only when Sally arrives), proceeds to talk about the activities that everyone will do while at the party.

Although the behaviours of both Bill and Sally were different, they each enjoyed the time just as much as the other.

Do you identify more with Sally or Bill?

PREFERENCE ONE

Work your way down the columns and read each adjacent statement to compare. Select one. You may want to choose both, however it is a forced choice. Which one do you prefer?

Choose from column **E** or **I** ...

E	I
☐ I have many friends	☐ I have a few close friends
☐ When people ask information about me, I'm willing to offer it	☐ Only my close friends really know me
☐ I consider myself a 'life of the party' at a gathering	☐ I prefer to let others take the lead at a gathering
☐ When meeting a group of new people, I like to introduce myself	☐ When meeting a group of new people, I prefer to be introduced by people I know
☐ In groups or meetings, I prefer to talk to express ideas	☐ In groups or meetings, I prefer to consider ideas before expressing them, then I may talk or not
☐ I am very sociable	☐ I am reserved, I may be friendly and congenial in a quiet manner
☐ I am gregarious and expressive and often outspoken	☐ I tend to be thoughtful
☐ I prefer to be out and about with a bunch of people	☐ I prefer to be on my own or with a few friends
☐ I am often quite willing to try new experiences	☐ I prefer the tried and true, and consider my actions

☐ I find when I am working on my own and by myself for a lengthy time, it tires me out	☐ I find when I am working with people, especially if I'm unfamiliar with them, for a lengthy time, it tires me out

Add the number of checks and total below...

E	I
TOTAL = / 10	TOTAL = / 10
_____	_____

Subtract the lowest from the highest which will result in the lettered preference you have chosen:

Highest Total _____ - Lowest Total _____ =

Number _____ _____ Matching Lettered Preference

(E or I)

Tie Breaker: If E = I write I

Preference Two
Buying A House

*T*wo partners, Mel and Jennifer are buying a house together. Mel walks into the living room and looks at the baseboard and thinks: 'Oh, look at the marks on the baseboard, the paint is chipped and worn'. Mel then looks at the ceiling and notices a stain: 'Oh, there must have been a leak in the roof, staining the ceiling' and automatically looks down at the floor to see any damage. Then Mel steps down to the basement and quickly sniffs the air discreetly: 'Oh, what a musty smell. There must be mold and dampness down here. And look at the furnace – it's as old as Moses and will probably cost money to repair'.

Jennifer walks into the living room and looks at the wall and thinks: 'Oh, wow. This is incredible. That wall will come down to make the living room and dining room into an open concept room'.

She then looks at the ceiling: 'Oh, turn this into a cathedral ceiling and the great room will be even more spacious looking'. Jennifer steps down to the basement: 'Oh, look at the size of this area! This will be a perfect playroom for the kids, even in later years. And the furnace will be replaced with a heat pump for future comfort and economical efficiency'.

Mel and Jennifer leave. After getting into their car, Mel says: "Do you believe that house? It's the worst we've ever seen!" - expecting agreement.

Jennifer says: "What?!? That's the best house we've seen. It will be perfect for us and the kids, even after years of living there!"

Do you identify more with Mel or Jennifer?

Paul Lamb

Preference Two

Work your way down the columns and read each adjacent statement to compare. Select one. You may want to choose both however it is a forced choice. Which one do you prefer?

Choose from column **S** or **N** …

S	N
☐ I prefer to first pay attention to details	☐ I prefer to first pay attention to the whole picture
☐ I prefer to deal with the concrete and keep my feet on solid ground	☐ I prefer to make things up and imagine
☐ I tend to consider the real rather than invent	☐ I tend to imagine and invent new ideas
☐ I prefer to live day to day and am less concerned about the future	☐ I prefer to live in the future and consider it more than today
☐ I prefer present satisfactions	☐ I prefer future achievements
☐ I tend to consider the here and now	☐ I tend to consider what's possible
☐ I tend to be realistic	☐ I tend to be idealistic
☐ I prefer to be literal	☐ I prefer to be metaphorical and symbolic
☐ I prefer to do what other people have done	☐ I prefer to be original
☐ I tend to live for enjoyment	☐ I tend to live for inspiration

Add the number of checks and total below...

S	N
TOTAL = / 10	TOTAL = / 10
_____	_____

Subtract the lowest from the highest which will result
in the lettered preference you have chosen:

Highest Total _____ - Lowest Total _____ =

Number _____ _____ Matched Lettered Preference

(S or N)

Tie Breaker: If S = N write N

PREFERENCE THREE
BUYING A CAR

*B*ev is looking at a car. She checks out the numbers and information stuck on the window of the car. She measures the wheelbase and looks at the statistics on the sheet. She thinks that the size of the wheelbase should give a comfortable ride. Bev opens the door without hesitation and sits in the driver's seat. Mulling over buying the car Bev thinks that it seats 5 people, 2 in the front, 3 in the back. The family is made up of 4 people. The car has climate control and can be changed precisely and accurately. The engine is large enough to provide acceleration and speed for safety. Bev thinks about it for 5 minutes and continues to review the stats sheet and adds up the pros and the cons. Since the car fits most of the needs Bev has calculated, she then decides to buy the car.

Gerry is looking at the same car. Gerry strolls around the car paying attention to the tires and the wheelbase. He feels the car will give the family a comfortable ride. He peers in the window and then opens the door and sits in the back seat. This car is roomy enough for the family to ride harmoniously. The car has climate control and that will definitely give a harmonious ride with the kids and his partner. Gerry likes this car- and it comes in the colour he likes. This car will give the family the ride to suit everyone. Gerry decides to buy the car.

Note: The same decision was reached by both Bev and Gerry. The mental processes that lead up to the decision was very different. If you need to, read the scenarios again, pay attention to the difference in the cognitive language. Bev took a very analytical and logical approach to the decision. Bev used statistics to help come to the conclusion. Gerry, on the other hand, took a very illogical and harmonious decision for the family - a warm and heartfelt conclusion.

Do you identify more with Bev or Gerry?

PREFERENCE THREE

Work your way down the columns and read each adjacent statement to compare. Select one. You may want to choose both however it is a forced choice. Which one do you prefer?

Choose from column **T** or **F** ...

T	F
☐ I tend to be very logical	☐ I tend to be circumstantial, consider values
☐ I am more interested in ideas and things	☐ I am more interested in people
☐ I tend to think about people	☐ I tend to feel about people
☐ I tend to analyze	☐ I tend to be sympathetic and empathetic
☐ I tend to be brief and business-like	☐ I tend to be friendly and sociable
☐ I prefer to organize information and then present clearly and briefly	☐ I tend to be unsure of where to start in presenting information, then present much information, & sometimes find myself rambling
☐ I tend to follow my head	☐ I tend to follow my heart
☐ I tend to critique	☐ I tend to appreciate
☐ I tend to be firm-minded	☐ I prefer to be tender-hearted
☐ I tend to question others' decisions	☐ I tend to agree with others' decisions

Add the number of checks and total below...

T	F
TOTAL = / 10	TOTAL = / 10
_____	_____

Subtract the lowest from the highest which will result
in the lettered preference you have chosen:

Highest Total _____ - Lowest Total _____ =

Number _____ _____ Matched Lettered Preference

(T or F)

Tie Breaker: If T = F write F

Preference Four
The Date

*C*hris and Sandy are talking with each other. Chris asks Sandy if she would like to go to the show next Friday. Sandy agrees that it would be a good idea. Chris plans the evening – the show starts at 7:00 p.m. "We need to be there at 6:45 at the latest to get a good seat and see the movie from the introductory credits. If we miss the beginning credits, there is no point in watching the movie! It takes 20 minutes to go from your place to the theatre. It takes me 15 minutes to go from my place to yours. So, I will leave my house at 6:10 p.m. Arrive at your house at 6:25. Then we will be in time for the show and get a good seat. So, be ready by 6:20 and give yourself an extra five minutes to do any forgotten odds and ends."

Next Friday comes around and Chris drives in the driveway at 6:24, and rings the doorbell. Sandy answers the door and is not dressed for the show. Sandy says "I don't feel like going to the show tonight, I'd rather go for a walk" After staring at Sandy, Chris says, "No way! We planned last week to go and that is what is going to happen. You can go to the show as you are. We have to leave now to get there on time." The argument between the two takes too much time to get to allow them to get to the show before the credits roll. There is no point in going to the movies so they go for a walk.

Do you identify more with Chris or Sandy?

PREFERENCE FOUR

Work your way down the columns and read each adjacent statement to compare. Select one. You may want to choose both however it is a forced choice. Which one do you prefer?

Choose from column **J** or **P** ...

J	P
☐ I tend to make 'to do' lists	☐ I prefer to avoid 'to do' lists and accomplish what needs doing
☐ I prefer being organized	☐ I prefer a free-flowing day
☐ I prefer deadlines	☐ I prefer to not to be constrained with deadlines
☐ I prefer to be scheduled	☐ I prefer to be adaptable to whatever comes along
☐ I tend to be decisive	☐ I tend to be curious
☐ I tend to be disciplined	☐ I prefer to be a free spirit
☐ I prefer to enjoy getting things done	☐ I prefer to start something new and let others finish
☐ I tend to prefer to have decisions made	☐ I tend to be a 'wait-and-see' person
☐ I prefer planning	☐ I prefer to improvise

Add the number of checks and total below...

J	P
TOTAL = / 10	TOTAL = / 10
_____	_____

Subtract the lowest from the highest which will result in the lettered preference you have chosen:

Highest Total _____ - Lowest Total _____ =

Number _____ _____Matching Lettered Preference

(J or P)

Tie Breaker: if J = P write P

The Four Lettered Preferences you have chosen are:

_____ _____ _____ _____

What do these letters mean? This is answered next.

Keep this information available to refer to later.

My type is INFJ. What is your type? Read the thumbnail descriptions below of your type. Do you agree with the brief description?

Read on...

PRLs of Wisdom*

Henry David Thoreau said:

"It takes two to speak the truth. One to speak, and another to listen."

Seven

Behaviour Patterns

The self-scoring charts match the columns below. The letter that received the highest score in each pair reveals your "preference".

	LEFT COLUMN	RIGHT COLUMN
PREFERENCE ONE HOW WE FOCUS AND GENERATE ENERGY	**E** XTROVERT	**I** NTROVERT
PREFERENCE TWO HOW WE GATHER INFORMATION	**S** ENSING	I **N** TUITIVE
PREFERENCE THREE HOW WE MAKE DECISIONS	**T** HINKING	**F** EELING

PREFERENCE FOUR HOW WE ACT IN THE WORLD	**J** UDGING	**P** ERCEIVING

To emphasize, we have all 8 preferences within us. They are dichotomous preferences and you fall somewhere on the continuum between the 2 preferences.

Preferences come from 4 continuums with 2 opposite letters on each. These are:

E/I - Extrovert/Introvert

The Extrovert and Introvert (E/I) Continuum describes from where we prefer to get our energy – how do we get energized when exhausted. Some people are mostly energized from outside themselves through other people or things – Extroverting. Some people are mostly energized from inside themselves – Introverting. Although we have both we prefer to use one more than the other.

S/N - Sensing/iNtuition

The Sensing and iNtuition (S/N) Continuum describes to what we prefer to pay attention. Some people mostly pay attention to details in the here and now – Sensing. Some people mostly pay attention to the big picture and are future oriented – iNtuitives. [The letter 'N' is used here as the letter 'I' is used previously with Introvert.] Although we have both we prefer to use one more than the other.

T/F - Thinking/Feeling

The Thinking and Feeling (T/F) Continuum describes how we prefer to make decisions or come to conclusion. Some people mostly make decisions through critical evaluation, logic, objectivity, laws or policies, firmness – Thinkers.

Some people mostly make decisions through values, harmony – Feelers. Although we have both we prefer to use one more than the other.

J/P - Judging/Perceiving

The Judging and Perceiving (J/P) Continuum describes how we are in the world. Some people are mostly planned, time oriented and scheduled with being organized as a core preference – Judging. Some people are mostly flexible, spontaneous and adaptable – Perceivers. Although we have both we prefer to use one more than the other.

Note: For more information see Appendix II, MBTI, The Constructive Use of Differences.

It is important to understand that the words Jung uses to describe the preferences are based in psychological rather than social terms. For example, Introvert (I) means something other than shy and reserved. It describes from where you get your energy. Judging preference means something other than being judgmental. It describes how you are in life. You may be characteristically shy or judgmental but the Jungian, and Myers and Briggs definitions place different meanings on words such as judgmental.

You are you. Rising above situations is best done by you. Everyone can rise above life altering circumstances especially by using the Iceberg Strategies such as these Jungian Personalities.

Understanding your type is like holding on to a cable for added support and strength, to have a perspective on yourself through life. Your greatest strength lies within. Your existing individual strength enables you to move through anything that comes your way. You are a vital person. The Iceberg Strategy - Jungian Personalities through the MBTI - provides a deep strategy with which you can strive to thrive by better knowing yourself and broadening our foundations for life.

PRLs of Wisdom*

Carl Gustav Jung said:

"The most terrifying thing is to accept oneself completely."

PERSONALITY TYPES – THUMBNAIL SKETCHES

Thank you to and Used by Permission
Source: http://www.ship.edu/~cgboeree/jung.html
Dr. C. George Boeree, Psychology Department,
Shippensburg University

Even without completing the questionnaire, you may very well recognize yourself in one or two of these types.

ENFJ (Extroverted feeling with intuiting): These people are easy speakers. They tend to idealize their friends. They make good parents, but have a tendency to allow themselves to be used. They make good therapists, teachers, executives, and salespeople.

ENFP (Extroverted intuiting with feeling): These people love novelty and surprises. They are big on emotions and expression. They are susceptible to muscle tension and tend to be hyper alert. They tend to feel self-conscious. They are good at sales, advertising, politics, and acting.

ENTJ (Extroverted thinking with intuiting): In charge at home, they expect a lot from spouses and kids. They like organization and structure and tend to make good executives and administrators.

ENTP (Extroverted intuiting with thinking): These are lively people, not humdrum or orderly. As mates, they are a little dangerous, especially economically. They are good at analysis and make good entrepreneurs. They do tend to play at one-upmanship.

ESFJ (Extroverted feeling with sensing): These people like harmony. They tend to have strong shoulds and should-nots. They may be dependent, first on parents and later on spouses. They wear their hearts on their sleeves and excel in service occupations involving personal contact.

ESFP (Extroverted sensing with feeling): Very generous and impulsive, they have a low tolerance for anxiety. They make good performers, they like public relations, and they love the phone. They should avoid scholarly pursuits, especially science.

ESTJ (Extroverted thinking with sensing): These are responsible mates and parents and are loyal to the workplace. They are realistic, down-to-earth, orderly, and love tradition. They often find themselves joining civic clubs!

ESTP (Extroverted sensing with thinking): These are action-oriented people, often sophisticated, sometimes ruthless - our "James Bonds." As mates, they are exciting and charming, but they have trouble with commitment. They make good promoters, entrepreneurs, and con artists.

INFJ (Introverted intuiting with feeling): These are serious students and workers who really want to contribute. They are private and easily hurt. They make good spouses, but tend to be physically reserved. People often think they are psychic. They make good therapists, general practitioners, ministers, and so on.

INFP (Introverted feeling with intuiting): These people are idealistic, self-sacrificing, and somewhat cool or reserved. They are very family and home oriented, but don't relax well. You find them in psychology, architecture, and religion, but never in business. Both Jung and I admire this type. Of course, both Jung and I are this type!

INTJ (Introverted intuiting with thinking): These are the most independent of all types. They love logic and ideas and are drawn to scientific research. They can be rather single-minded, though.

INTP (Introverted thinking with intuiting): Faithful, preoccupied, and forgetful, these are the bookworms. They tend to be very precise in their use of language. They are good at logic and math and make good philosophers and theoretical scientists, but not writers or salespeople.

ISFJ (Introverted sensing with feeling): These people are service and work oriented. They may suffer from fatigue and tend to be attracted to troublemakers. They are good nurses, teachers, secretaries, general practitioners, librarians, middle managers, and housekeepers.

ISFP (Introverted feeling with sensing): They are shy and retiring, are not talkative, but like sensuous action. They like painting, drawing, sculpting, composing, dancing - the arts generally - and they like nature. They are not big on commitment.

ISTJ (Introverted sensing with thinking): These are dependable pillars of strength. They often try to reform their mates and other people. They make good bank examiners, auditors, accountants, tax examiners, supervisors in libraries and hospitals, business, home etc., and phys. ed. teachers, and boy or girl scouts!

ISTP (Introverted thinking with sensing): These people are action-oriented and fearless, and crave excitement. They are impulsive and dangerous to stop. They often like strategies, instruments, and weapons, and often become technical experts. They are not interested in communications and are often incorrectly diagnosed as dyslexic or hyperactive. They tend to do badly in school.

EIGHT

HOLDING ON TO WHO I AM

What does knowing this MBTI information do for me and you? It enables us to deliberately choose one preference over the other. We can thrive in different situations by using each preference or type useful in any situation. We are enabled to hold on to who each of us is. We use our strength and wisdom in different situations.

I know this by knowing my right and left hand strengths. I use the personality type the same way. The MBTI tells me where my preferences are and what I prefer – such as, how I gain energy when it is diminished and what I need to do to reenergize (I am an Introvert so I know I need alone time rather than being with a gang of people and socializing). Being with people can be more exhausting. It also tells me I'm not being antisocial, I am simply regaining my energy. And that takes a weight off my shoulders!

The MBTI strategy by enables us to:

- Become more self-aware and broaden our foundations for personal, professional and organization growth

- Articulate and identify our strengths

- Identify our challenges without hiding behind them

- Use the 'constructive use of differences'

- Maintain our life's balance

- Strive to Thrive

- Enable us to Explore the Iceberg

NINE

BALANCING TYPE
BEING AN INFJ

To emphasize, we all have the 4 pairs of preferences within us. We prefer one preference out of each pair. This creates our own type. My four preferences, or my type, is INFJ.

Extrovert / **I**ntrovert - Energy

Recall, Extroverts gain energy from outside themselves, through other people or things. Introverts gain energy from within themselves. I am an Introvert.

Advantage as an Introvert - sample

- Early on in my recovery, I didn't like myself and compared myself with others. I wanted to stay away from people. As an Introvert, this was easy for me to do.

Disadvantages as an Introvert - sample

- As an Introvert, it was easy for me, on my own, to dwell in my dark mindful cave of desolation. Being in my cave of desolation allowed my Black and White Thinking to trounce all over me!

Balancing my Extrovert / Introvert Preferences

- When I needed to Extrovert myself, even after taking only baby steps outside my Zone of Comfort, my energy waned. To replenish my energy, to fight the good fight, I knew to Introvert myself and go inside myself to recharge.

- When my Black and White Thinking was taking charge of me, I knew it was time to Extrovert myself and talk with good people, like health care staff, sharing challenges with co-patients and others, and family and close friends.

- I Extroverted myself to overcome my social imbalance.

- My injury uses up much of my energy just to exist. Extroverting myself depletes it even more so which creates huge fatigue.

- All in all, to recharge my batteries, I knew to go within to gain energy to go without.

- Extroversion is not my preference; I still needed to talk with therapists, psychologists, physicians and the like. To open up with professionals, I slid on over the continuum to Extrovert myself (Extroverts are chatty and people like that – Extroverts seem friendly). I was afraid of being ostracized, the second greatest fear in life, because I felt myself to be a loser and mentally challenged. I wanted desperately for people to like me so I would feel I belonged. I needed to avoid my cave of desolation. I became chatty, too chatty, in retrospect. When I Extroverted myself it was hard work and I became very tired. Coupled with the exhaustion from my Acquired Brain Injury, fatigue overwhelmed me. This was a triple whammy. I was tired from my brain injury putting my body through extra work simply to function; I put myself through work to Extrovert myself.

Then at the end of the day when I spent time with my children, I couldn't focus, talk well, think straight and just be with my children. I went to my dominant Introvert, rather than *cave in,* I simply *'caved away'* from everyone including my children. I did not feel like the dad I so wanted to be!

Sensing/i**N**tuition

Recall, Sensors look at details, focusing on the here-and-now. iNtuitives look at the big picture, focusing on the future.

Advantages as an i**N**tuitive - sample

- INtuitives tend to look at the big picture and are future-oriented. Sensing people tend to consider pieces of the big picture and are often in the here-and-now. I used my 'big picture', as an iNtuitive, to see myself as a whole person rather than focusing on my individual challenges. This detracted my thinking from being a broken and incomplete man.

- I thought of my future to set goals for myself and considered all the possibilities.

Disadvantages as an i**N**tuitive - sample

- I avoided the individual and broken pieces of my life rather than focusing on them and working to fix them in the present.

Balancing My **S**ensing / i**N**tuitive Preferences

- I used my sensing to live day to day - not to be troubled with the unknown and vast uncertainty of my future.

- I avoided my future troubles and struggles, which allowed me to view my goals that I created using my Intuition.

- When there was and is trauma in my life I switch to my Sensing to think of the day-to-day operations rather than the future possibilities. To live one day at a time to avoid the possible dismal future (Black and White Thinking)

- Using my Sensing, I encourage 'one-thing-at-a-time' mode of living

- To consider what challenge I could work on by itself to create a bigger picture – to become a complete man again

- Because I often believed I had no future life, I welcomed life by shortening it to one day rather than weeks, months or years.

- This is where I did the flip-flop. There are daily goals (Sensing) as well as future goals (iNtuition). When doing physiotherapy, I focused on the pieces of my puzzle, using my least preferred sensing, to focus on my individual challenges to improve them daily. This enabled me to better expect the big picture (preferred iNtuition) of my recovery – to reach my goal.

Thinking / **F**eeling - Decisions

Recall, Thinkers critique, analyze and are logical. Feelers prefer harmony, values, and are attracted to people.

Advantages as **F**eeling Preference - sample

- To consider what's right with the situation as opposed to dwelling on what's wrong with my life.

Disadvantages of **F**eeling Preference - sample

- Wanting to be liked and be attached to others with a fear of being ostracized. I recognized this fear when I returned to work.

- Listening to music with the radio playing a myriad of romantic and heart-wrenching songs.

- Prefer harmony in my life when there isn't any, which was brought on by my Black and White Thinking.

Balancing my **T**hinking / **F**eeling Preferences:

- When I want to be blue I turn to my Feeling preference that supports my emotions. This is not to imply that Thinkers do not get sad. Their sadness is less than Feeling preference or short term. Thinkers tend to be logical in their emotional pursuit that may make them appear void of emotion.

- To control the time and situation for this to happen, I deliberately choose the 80/20 Rule to flow in and out of Feeling and Thinking.

- I choose appropriate times to be sad and forlorn, like watching a sad movie or listening to a sad song. Perhaps even when I want to feel sorry for myself. I do this on my own. I found myself drawn to Thinkers who usually have little time for this.

- To detach myself pondering my losses, from the trauma, and otherwise, in my life.

- Using my Thinking, to be detached from ones who were lovingly in my life and are no longer. I use my Thinking preference to detach myself from those situations that impact on my heartfelt pain.

- To become cold hearted if necessary, which I don't like to do but I do to protect myself.

- After being in my Thinking preference for as long as I need, I return to the strength of my Feeling preference.

Judging / **P**erceiving - Action

Recall, Judgers are scheduled, desire closure, are timely and orderly. Perceivers are adaptable, and spontaneous.

Advantages of My **J**udging Preference - sample

- As a Judger I prefer closure and have done several things that put closure on my injury, notwithstanding it will be with me forever. Writing this book is one example. Helping others help themselves gives me value and enables me to place closure and let go of feeling less-than-nothing.

- As a Judger, and therefore a timekeeper, when I exercise, especially, walking and running, I tend to use a stopwatch. For example, run for one minute then walk for one minute then I run.

Following is one small and concrete example, exercising, of how life is founded on type – your strength.

When I decided to start running again (when I could run, at least a little bit), I used my type (INFJ) foundationally. As an Introvert, I run by myself. This reenergizes me, even if I am running! This allows me to tap into my N (iNtuitive) and I dream of what's possible and imagine. Running moves into my Feeling and satisfies my values for health. I use my J (Judging) to guide my running. Perceivers often listen to their body more than a watch. If I used my Perceiving preference and was spontaneous listening to my body, I would have quit running - it's too hard; my body's tired; I'm tired. My stopwatch put closure on my running and encouraged me to persevere. Stubborn?!? No. I persevere!

Disadvantages of My **J**udging Preference - sample

- As Judging preference, it is hard having an Acquired Brian Injury. One of the symptoms of my injury is being disorganized. I was very organized before coma. Now I look at my workplace to organize it and have no clue what to do. Is that what it is like for Perceivers? I always thought that organizing their desk was simply not a priority – or they see it organized when 'Js' see a mess.

Balancing my **J**udging / **P**erceiving Preferences:

- I use my Perceiving preference and become adaptable to whatever comes along to deal with my disorganizing symptom from my injury. I consider and hear myself say 'whatever'. This is a tough one for me because even looking at a disorganized space is very hard, especially, when the 'before' Paul was very organized, sometimes considered anal!

- The Perceiving preference complements my day-to-day living when I use my Sensing by being adaptable and spontaneous to what ever comes along each day.

- It can be said that I 'J'-myself and plan to be a P

Since Judging is my preference and where I feel strong, I do small things to "J" myself. I may organize my pantry, even when "P"'s would say it's organized enough. Simply wearing a stopwatch helps me feel like a Judger!

It isn't easy being an INFJ. Of all types, INFJ's are the rarest, particularly males.

Rising above situations is best done by you. Everyone can rise above life altering circumstances especially by using the Iceberg Strategies. Using your type will make your growth unique.

The prescription invites you to slide over on the preference continuum, if your preferences are different, to use your ESTP.

I have to slide over on each preference continuum as this type is opposite to me - INFJ.

This means my prescription is challenging for me to do early on. The work required is valuable as it helps digest my pound-of-dirt.

I am not suggesting that you purge yourself of your preferences (although it can't be done; the personality theory explains you are born with your type). Your type is comprised of your Preferences - your strengths. Trying to be another type is successful only for a short time - you can only be someone else for a limited time.

ESTP

Extroverted Preference:

No one is an island. In troubling times, especially, it is important and necessary to share and talk about our challenges – our pound-of-dirt. We may need to Extrovert ourselves to talk with someone, like a therapist whom we do not really know, rather than talking to a close friend. Being an Introvert I usually confide in those whom I know are trustworthy.

Sensing Preference:

Often in distraught times there doesn't seem to be any future or great possibilities. In the extreme we think of suicide when the future seems lost or miserable or the feeling that suicide is the only choice, as I did. Dealing with a small piece of time, like a day, you are able to cope better than dealing with a longer future, particularly when life is overwhelming and unmanageable. Use Sensing Preference to live one day at a time.

Thinking Preference:

To avoid emotions altogether is rather unlikely. Emotions are there but in Thinkers, they tend to dwell on them less. To Thinkers emotions tend not to be logical. Use your Thinking Preference to detach yourself from any distraught circumstance. Think logically about a situation where your social feelings seem to cloud the situation.

Perceiving Preference:

Often in the pound-of-dirt times there is no closure. For example, in my situation it was never determined how the car crash happened. For me this would have helped to put closure on my trauma. Many distraught times never find closure. Perceivers adapt. Using this preference is useful for that reason – adapt to whatever happens.

Using my Perceiving preference I taught myself how to let go, for example, of my trauma. Hanging on is sometimes the worst that can happen. We do ourselves disfavour. It hurts us Feeling types. It's often like hanging on to a ghost.

Summary Prescription
ESTP

EXTROVERSION

Go outside yourself; talk things out with a therapist, friend, rather than torturing yourself by only 'thinking things through'. No one is an island.

SENSING:

Live day-to-day rather than considering the distant future; often in thoughts during depressed times there is no future.

THINKING:

Be detached, and cold-hearted, if need be, to protect you from painful heartaches.

PERCEIVING:

Be spontaneous and adaptable to whatever comes along. As mentioned, it complements the Sensing day-to-day attentions. Needing to be planned and organized is not necessarily helpful when it is you yourself facing the unknown.

Will this prescription help avoid self-harm behaviour?

TEN

THE DYNAMICS AND SYNERGY OF THE ICEBERG STRATEGIES

The Iceberg Strategies, collectively, are greater than the sum of their parts. The diagram, Balancing Life, illustrates the precariousness and the delicate balance of each of our lives, professions and organizations. For example, when we as individuals or as organizations are overwhelmed then we are thrown off balance. We need to move into our strengths at various times to regain our balance.

This is based in and on each of us being responsible for our own lives. Each of us make it a wonderful life or otherwise. Balancing Life is balanced on each of us. We are solely responsible for who we are, how we manage ourselves and what we make of life, including unexpected circumstances.

I live life and balance it through my type. My Foundations – Mind, Body, Spirit – are all fed through my type to enable me to digest my pound-of-dirt and go beyond surviving to thriving! The Ingredients – exercise, family, community, work – feed the Foundations.

We are complex and hard to explain. However, within that complexity is the certainty of simplicity. It is so counter-intuitive and this simply complex notion makes life brim with generosity. The synergistic process is more than linear. It is as a silky spider web. The Ingredients and Foundational elements reach out and touch, support, and strengthen each other. It is a win-learn situation. How we think is the determining factor.

It is vital to understand that there is no failure only feedback. Because the Foundations and Ingredients all support each other, this is the reason why when one door closes another one opens. The Foundations and Ingredients are the doors within our lives. And these doors are all linked together. Focusing on the closed door may stop us in our tracks.

We may allow the closed door to blind us. We may prefer to be blind for 20% of the time and ask 'why did this happen to me?' "It wasn't my fault. Someone else closed the door." We may need to use our Venting Valve for a time and then choose to move on.

If someone else did close the door then that is a turning point in your life. Now it is up to you to create and manage your choice points. It is time to move to the remaining 80% - what can I do now? When can I do it? This will open your mind and eyes to move forward and search for and magnify the door that has been waiting for you to open. Magnifying the door will make it a bigger part of your life and perhaps overwhelm the closed door.

Was the door even closed? Was it Black and White Thinking that said the door had been closed, when it wasn't? Perhaps the door was still ajar, but perhaps our extreme Black and White Thinking said it was closed.

When we are in the 80% zone of solutions we are increasing the size of our Zone of Comfort. When we are in our enlarged Zone of Comfort, using our type, we work comfortably and strongly and our attitude reaches a greater height, then we are enabled to walk on troubled waters. Attitude reaches out for challenges to become strengths.

Balancing Life is balancing on and founded in type - whatever your type may be.

SYNERGISM OF TYPE

Exercising provides a healthy mind and body to provide for all ingredients within the Foundations. When all ingredients are doing well they provide encouragement to continue exercising. Success breeds success. This influences perceptions and primes the mind to do its best thinking.

The Foundations – example of exercising

Mind – I'm considering I need to exercise. From what I learn and observe this is a good decision (Introvert myself and think things through). This may be my perceptions looking at what they want to see. However, my Black and White Thinking is not involved which gives me trust in my thinking.

Body – I exercise and maintain a healthy intake based on my type (INFJ) which is Introverted for exercising (on my own), iNtuitive for a healthy future, Feeling as it makes me feel good which are also my values and Judging for food management (schedule and record what and when I eat and drink).

Spirit – I think more clearly through a healthy body that increases my belief in myself. This feeds a healthier attitude. My belief in a Higher Power (F) increases my desire to keep my thinking clear to maintain my healthiness leading back to a greater increase in self-efficacy and attitude.

Eleven

Exploring The Iceberg
The Top Ten

To help enable you to Explore the Iceberg, in the following top TEN choose and circle one number from 10 to 1.

PRLs of Wisdom*

The Koran says:

"Do you think you shall enter the garden of bliss without such trials as came to those who have passed before you?"

ON A SCALE OF 10 TO 1...

1. ...where 10 is always and 1 is the opposite, I ask questions of my self and others, starting with the words: 'how', or 'when', or 'where', or 'what' rather than 'why'.

    1   2   3   4   5   6   7   8   9   10

2. ...where 10 is appropriately responsible and 1 is the opposite, I broaden my attitude using the Venting Valve to include 80% or more optimistic and empowering thoughts over 20% or less negative and disempowering thoughts.

    1   2   3   4   5   6   7   8   9   10

3. ...where 10 is appropriately responsible time spent and 1 is the opposite, I create a healthy body by my actions and by my intake.

    1   2   3   4   5   6   7   8   9   10

4. ...where 10 is always and 1 is the opposite, I have explored both poles on my MBTI preference continuum.

    1   2   3   4   5   6   7   8   9   10

5. ...where 10 is all the time and 1 is the opposite, I know when my rationalizations overtake me, which enables me to counteract them.

    1   2   3   4   5   6   7   8   9   10

6. ...where 10 is always and 1 is the opposite, I can stop myself from being pushed around by the 'blame game' and take complete responsibility for circumstances in my life.

    1   2   3   4   5   6   7   8   9   10

7. ...where 10 is totally and 1 is the opposite, I take ownership for my life to stabilize it, take reasonable risks to expand my Zone of Comfort.

    1   2   3   4   5   6   7   8   9   10

8. ...where 10 is all the time and 1 is the opposite; I make appropriately responsible decisions.

    1   2   3   4   5   6   7   8   9   10

9. ...where 10 is all the time and 1 is the opposite, I take responsible risks, if needed, to expand my comfort zone.

    1   2   3   4   5   6   7   8   9   10

10. ...where 10 is always and 1 is the opposite, I am absorbing this book and/or others that complement it to Explore the Iceberg

    1   2   3   4   5   6   7   8   9   10

Scoring Averages:

☐   9-10:   Consider yourself a Zen-like master.

☐   8:   Surface for air, rest, then return to Exploring the Iceberg

☐   5-7:   Go ahead, feel the fear and do it anyway. Delve under the surface and do some exploring. Your ambivalence is getting in the way. You have appropriately responsible strength and wisdom.

☐   2-4:   There is more to the Iceberg than the tip – ask the Titanic.

☐   0-1:   There is a tip to the Iceberg to explore and start growing (read the book).

What will you be doing to move up on each scale by 1?

PRLs of Wisdom*

Ralph Waldo Emerson said

"What lies behind us and what lies before us are tiny matters compared to what lies within us."

V

THE STORY OF
STRENGTH
AND
WISDOM

**STRIVE
TO
THRIVE**

PRLs of Wisdom*

Exploring the Iceberg broadens the foundation of your strength and wisdom -- Strive to Thrive

ONE

THE MYTH OF THE POUND-OF-DIRT

What is the benefit of Exploring the Iceberg?

You are full of stories. Your stories make you who you are by your interpretations if them. Harness your stories, hold on to them, learn from them and create who you want to be. Find the strength in your stories. Rather than denying what occurred magnify how you can use it to be the best for the world.

My story from coma to thriving and the Iceberg Strategies provide appropriate information to enable you, your family, your profession and your organization to grow even when facing challenges. It can raise you up to be more than the sum of your parts - synergy.

In fact, in time, what you see as a challenge now you can change it into a strength - Remember, **it's not the event it's the perception of the event** that matters and holds the foundation for your thoughts. This is the germ of Constructive Challenges. Your experiences give you stories from which to learn. There is no failure, only feedback.

Some of your past stories may hold you responsible for your inappropriate behaviour such as pushing people around for your advantage, drug dependency, murder, and the entire continuum of inappropriate behaviours. Or, some of your past stories may hold nasty things, some of that pound-of-dirt that has been done to you. It may even be an event coming from Mother Nature! If your learning focuses on inappropriate behaviour, do something differently.

In any kind of relationship, agreement all the time is almost impossible. However, the smoothness comes in understanding the other and yourself. You may both need the other's points of view.

There is 'your' story; there is the 'other's' story; and there is 'our' story, the strongest story. Perhaps one is talking about what is wrong and the other person is talking about what is right about a situation. Perhaps one person is both simply talking about the same story with two sides.

You know that neither of you are being deliberately obstreperous. You know this because you both have genuinely grown because both of you are in the same organization or family. You have passed false growth and created an organization of respect, dignity, value and understanding.

First and foremost, Exploring the Iceberg is using the Iceberg Strategies like Myers-Briggs Type Indicator enable you to go deeper with knowledge and wisdom. The Strategies enable delivery of your many strengths, needs, wants, and challenges to the world at large by balancing your life which is founded in your type.

It is not as though you say to your challenges, 'I'm ready, come and get me!' You know how to manage your challenges because you deal with them in your strengths. You can feel the fear and do it anyway! You are increasing the size of your Zone of Comfort. Your paradigms can shift.

It is a different way to think. This way of thinking enables you to become stronger and wiser.

When you come to challenges in life, P.E.P. Talk can get behind and inside you. Put Perseverance behind Effort and hold them together with Patience..

Changing your thinking and language bolsters your strength and wisdom. This is the way to carve out what works and magnify your optimism and expectations to set them free.

From the many choices you have made to increase your personal control, your personal power increases your self-efficacy creating an attitude that will keep growing in positive directions for both you and others.

Making you stronger and wiser makes your family and organization stronger and wiser, which makes you stronger and wiser.

Round and round and round it goes

Where it stops nobody knows.

Before, your workplace may have told you to leave your life at the door and come in and do your job! Now, because your whole life is stronger and wiser which is contributing to the organization, it will insist you bring in all of you, because it needs the whole you.

You create your life by the interpretation of your stories. This book invites you to be responsible for yourself, your profession and your organization. Many leaders espouse the same adage yet one of our spiritual leaders throughout time said it best when speaking to physicians, paraphrased here.

"Heal yourselves!"

As it has been said, no one is an island. No one is self-sufficient. We need others. We need to get along with folks - it starts with us.

Each of us chooses to move forward or not. Each of us accepts or does not accept support and help from others. No matter how much help we get, we first need to welcome it; accept it; learn how to move forward when it is accepted.

There is darkness or a pound-of-dirt in everyone's life. In our darkness we sometimes feel we are standing still or moving backwards. That happens and has to happen. It is like finding a light to shine in the darkness.

You create synergy; it's not created for you.

Balancing Life and growing starts and ends with you. You accept and digest your pound-of-dirt. You are the Alpha and Omega of your life.

Rather than denying any darkness in our lives the Iceberg Strategies assist moving through our darkness. Once you effectively use these Iceberg Strategies, you will be responding with the question:

"What dirt?"

I have been and still am Exploring the Iceberg. At the beginning of this book an invitation was put out to raise your bar of survival and strive to thrive. A second invitation is now at hand. It is an invitation to create and develop your own or more of your own Iceberg Strategies.

It is a journey. Am I simply doing what I ought to be doing? I am.

TWO

MOTIVATION

High regard for people is fundamental to me and this book. Each of us equally has appropriately responsible strengths and wisdom. Each of us probably draws from different sources, like our individual Personality Type, but we have equally that strength and wisdom within us. Rising above situations is best done by you. Everyone can rise above life altering circumstances especially by using the information provided in Exploring the Iceberg. You, as well, have something significant yet to do.

The first step to motivating yourself to meet any challenge is to change your mind. Whatever your thoughts and feelings are that block your progress, simply change your mind to initiate movement. You can be stopping yourself from progressing by your thoughts.

Everyone is motivated. The 'gene' of motivation is in everybody. People are motivated to do what they want to do, not necessarily what you want them to do.

Motivation comes from within; some reasons are:

When the rewards of a task are personally relevant, personal relevance often relates to your type. Because your task resonates with your type, you are motivated to take it on. (Remember, however, anyone can do anything in crisis or if absolutely necessary.)

When your motivated behaviour is working in strengths, when your behaviour falls within your dominant preference, you have more confidence, strength and energy – behaviour in your type usually creates greater self-efficacy. Past experience shows results and success breeds success. Your motivation becomes greater than the sum of its parts.

When you both understand what is expected, when speaking to another and using their language, you both become very clear and better understood. (Note: for Language see Appendix III – Communication and Language.)

You do what you want to do and so does everyone else. When you communicate your wants and needs in the other's language there is a greater possibility for recognizing you are both on the same page. Often you both want the same thing but are describing it differently.

Motivation comes from within to achieve your desires within you and without you. Hence, being motivated to Explore the Iceberg is your choice. You are invited to activate your 'motivation gene' for the journey.

If this is new thinking for you, notice how changing your mind can create forward motion toward success.

How do you change your mind? Consider different thoughts (one example is, rather than thinking – 'that won't work' think 'how could that work?'), use different language and talk with others who have this language that have forward motion toward success. And, believe in yourself. Know you have the strength and wisdom for accomplishments. (Note: for Language see Appendix III – Communication and Language.)

How do you believe in yourself? Step one would be to begin using the Iceberg Strategies. That's where I started when I had no belief in myself. I started at the tip of my Iceberg.

The invitation of this book is to use it appropriately and responsibly. It's your choice as to how it is put into operation. Exploring the Iceberg for greater self-awareness will harness your brain for you, your profession, and your organization to grow. You simply need to change your mind to start to harness your motivation to thrive.

Three

Thriving

It is often, if not always, a goal of individuals and organizations to make money, and that is assumed in this book. The meaning of going beyond competition is focusing on today to create tomorrow. It means focusing on each and every person to create your desired organization or family.

Going beyond competition *can* happen with the Iceberg Strategies. Is it possible for everyone to make money, enjoy the work, enjoy the workplace, their family and be passionate?

Passion can happen when individuals think and feel they are heard, understood and especially valued and shown respect by the organization. When this happens, value and respect run rampant. A passionate person will be compelled and enthusiastic about the effort needed to be productive. Greater production often means more money.

When people gain satisfaction in their organization, it can catapult profits and expand production to beyond imagination.

The business of big or small organizations or families is to produce, profit and anchor neighbourhoods, cities, provinces/states, country. Go within to perform without. Internal growth leads to external production. Go beyond competition to create the best organization.

PRLs of Wisdom*

Continue the journey of you. Feel the Fear and Do it Anyway.

Those who most need delve below the surface, tend to stay at the tip of the Iceberg...

FOUR

EMERGING YOUR SELF-ESTEEM

When I came out of my coma at mid-life like a six year old, I had no self-esteem, no confidence, no worth or value. I was lower than a snake's belly. Using the Iceberg Strategies my self-esteem began to emerge.

Knowing yourself deeply is the bedrock of self-esteem.

Everyone has the same core strength deep within. Self-esteem is on a continuum. Your self-esteem falls on that continuum different than anyone else. More precisely, you have enabled your self-esteem to fall there. You are not given high or low self-esteem. Everyone has equal shares. And like everyone else, your self-esteem is bursting to come forth – overflowing its brim.

Influences

Yet most people keep their self-esteem hidden and repressed. What each person manifests as their self-esteem is limited or bounded by many factors. Although not inclusive some of the limitations come from the following influences.

It is more difficult when you have valueless outside support or blockages such as from your upbringing and from bullies intimidating you. It is almost impossible to enable your self-esteem to emerge, when this happens at younger ages. Simply put, you are too young to understand it. You are *just* learning about yourself and life.

The ability to enable your self-esteem to emerge starts at birth – yet there is no independent learning. We rely on our upbringing. Valueless support at the start is a dire disadvantage. In fact, expectantly, you don't even realize it when growing up that parents or guardians are repressing you. It is assumed most parents or guardians raise their children as best they can with what they've got. None-the-less, every kid is still repressed. Albeit, some are repressed more than others; some more intensely than others; and the repression has a greater impact on some than others.

You are taught to respect your parents and elders. This is confused culturally and religiously. The confusion comes that respecting parents and elders is synonymous with them always being right or knowing better. Compounding this repression is, you learn what you live. Growing up with repression you tend to carry your learning with you, internalize it, and it culminates in oppressing yourself.

You live life feeling you have no value. In reality, you have great value, as everyone does. You just may not know it, yet. Fortunately, emerging your self-esteem and your personal growth can start at any age.

Let's be clear. Some people are bullies and braggarts as this gets them what they want. This is what they have learned and what works for them, and is used in their lifetime in different ways depending on such characteristics as age, position and gender. These reasons and rationalizations may be unlimited. Some like to bully people. Others are afraid they will be seen as bullies – such individuals only eek out their self-esteem from fear of the judgement of others.

Some manifest their self-esteem fraudulently. Some have low self-esteem and hide it, mostly form themselves. Aggressive behaviours, as mentioned above (and add your own), intimidate others. It shows the aggressors what they believe is strength and self-esteem., fraudulent as it is. It actually hides their strength and wisdom.

Some people interpret their self-esteem with their position in society or career. If they are 'powerful' positions as defined by culture or are seen as financially wealthy, they assume they *must* have high self-esteem. For example, when someone is unable to admit they are wrong or that no one else knows better, this is a manifestation of their low self-esteem filtered through their mask.

Personally, when I was in denial of my trauma and turning point, it was because my self-esteem was so low I had to protect myself. I denied what happened to me so as not to be wrong and fragile – though I was in both instances.

Most people exaggerate their level of self-esteem, no matter their position or age. Society has interpreted that if you are short on self-esteem then short on confidence you have little value. What is usually missed is the strength the individual actually has that is different from anyone else. Your strengths are unique and individual to you. Not focusing on strengths is immoral and unethical.

Sometimes individuals avoid Exploring the Iceberg for fear of finding out the truth about themselves (see also Part III Chapter Four). Becoming deeply self-aware, they discover, they are showing little self-esteem. It is diluted and masked by their bravado. This is their challenge – to know themselves deeply to become self-aware – and discover their genuine self-esteem.

Culture has identified and misinterpreted too much self-esteem as unhealthy behaviour. Some people are afraid that showing too much self-esteem may be seen as arrogance or boasting. Some define it as bullying. This comes from not knowing *how* to show their self-esteem. Again, we do not learn, see or discover what healthy self-esteem looks like growing up. Often learning to be, for example, assertive comes about as an adult, usually, and then the unhealthy manifestation of self-esteem is ingrained and needs or sometime needs to be first unlearned.

Some are bullied or pushed around and this keeps their self-esteem repressed. Such a one has no confidence through emotional and/or physical abuse and other psychological impacts. These people have no belief in themselves, no self-efficacy (belief in yourself) and this cruelly interferes with them emerging their self-esteem. No matter the language used, bullied as a kid or pushed around as an adult, it all stems from their self-esteem or self-efficacy. The bully and the bullied both have little self-esteem showing it in their own different ways.

Responsibility is a two way street. Some individuals blame the bully or someone else for their low self-esteem. And that is normal thinking. Being pushed around is reprehensible and simply not right. The bullied person gets into the blame game. Yet only blaming the bully takes responsibility away from the bullied to emerge their self-esteem.

Some are afraid to have their self-esteem emerge because they may have to take action and *do* something in the world or within themselves. Disabling the emergence of their self-esteem gives them permission for someone else to look after them. This is a tool used to absolve them of taking any self-responsibility.

Some have not been taught how to emerge their self-esteem – perhaps their parents or guardians, themselves have little self-esteem due to not having learned how to emerge their own self-esteem and so unable to teach another. These folks need read this book – <u>Exploring the Iceberg</u>. Or perhaps they don't want to have lower self-esteem than their offspring (this can happen subconsciously). So the cycle of low self-esteem continues from generation to generation.

Knowing yourself deeply is the bedrock of self-esteem and is the primary reason we are here -- To love and respect ourselves to enable us to love and respect another without feeling pushed around or bullied.

The Iceberg Strategies process your journey to explore who you are deeply, to really get to know yourself deep within. The Strategies inherently invite you to know your genuine self-esteem and appropriately emerge it in your life without hurt to yourself or others.

Truthful Eyes

In the course of Exploring the Iceberg you are discovering the truth. The deeper you know yourself the more truth you expose to emerge your self-esteem to launch your undeniable freedom. The truth is revealed more the deeper you go to know yourself. It may seem like a never ending journey. This makes it the best reason to start today. The more and more truth you discover the freer to become.

How does the truth set you free?

Knowing yourself deeply is the bedrock of self-esteem. The more self-esteem you uncover and use in your life, the more confidence you garner to be the real you! When you have this, your self-value and self-worth increase for you to have the strength, courage and wisdom to view the world and yourself though truthful eyes.

At the same time respecting the cultural civilities in which you live, your truthful eyes see without wearing the cultural masks. You see what others want you to be to get what they want. You have the strength and wisdom to be both the same and different – to be part of a group or culture and, at the same time, to be on your own – an individual. When this happens you find balance in your life. Your self-respect comes outward to respect others. This enables you to see the value and worth in others without fear of being undermined or dominated in life.

Spiritual leaders call this 'love'.

You know who you are deeply. You enable yourself to clearly know and articulate who you are and what you want in life. This enables you to grab onto what you want and leave the rest behind. Your life is less burdensome and filled with abundance. You enable yourself to be set free.

The primary reason you are here is to know yourself deeply. The secondary reason you are here is yours to explore. It's your choice.

This will be discussed in the next chapter – Favourable Junctures. Through the Iceberg Strategies you make visible your invisible Favourable Junctures.

PRLs of Wisdom*

*Knowing yourself deeply is the
bedrock of self-esteem ...*

FIVE

FAVOURABLE JUNCTURES

Once I had accepted my trauma as treasure, my Favourable Junctures became evident. Favourable Junctures are invisible possibilities and opportunities here for the taking everyday, all the time. Your Favourable Junctures are waiting patiently for you to make them visible. As Yogi Bera said, 'when you come to a fork in the road, you have to take it'.

Favourable Junctures become visible at each level of exploration. They often come forth as epiphanies – the aha's of life. It is like riding in a retail elevator of life. You know who you are and what you want so you know where to go, what floor to get off on to get it and leave the rest behind. Life is filled with abundance and is less burdensome.

The elevator analogy is indicative of our society-at-large and our limited language. This understandable metaphor that paints a word picture is – riding *up* in an elevator. Our society refers to *rising* to the top to reach success. We use the analogy of going *up* to heaven and *down* to hell. The analogy here falls into the same limiting language. It is the language and analogy we have been raised on and understand. It describes going *up* in an elevator *outside* of us when self-esteem refers to going *down* deeply *inside* of us.

Exploring the Iceberg – the metaphor for life – is knowing yourself deeply to discover your true self-esteem, worth and value. This initiates your strength and wisdom to know what you are to do here on earth.

Favourable Junctures are always there but are invisible to you. You may see them Juncture; yet, you do not perceive it as Favourable. You pass it by because you are looking in the wrong direction with less self-awareness or you are not ready to see it. Favourable Junctures are at your service when you are ready to see them – when you know yourself more deeply vis-à-vis your current stage of life. Your higher power and/or the universe (whatever your stance) know when you are ready to make visible your Favourable Junctures. Like 'one person's trash (pound-of-dirt) is another person's treasure'.

In my trauma, I initially perceived my injury as a pound-of-dirt and denied it, wanted to discard it or run away from it. I ran away from Exploring the Iceberg. Yet, counter-intuitive to my thinking at the time, Exploring the Iceberg, was a Favourable Juncture waiting for me. I avoided making it visible, as I was not ready for my self-awareness to perceive it as such. I didn't even know what Exploring the Iceberg was.

We have created a *healthy* rationalization by thinking and saying that 'things happen for a reason'. And the above description is the reason. Since challenges happen in our life and rationalizing that they are there for a reason invites us to Explore the Iceberg and to learn from that event. Recall there is no failure, only feedback. The only failure is to avoid Exploring the Iceberg.

The more I Explored the Iceberg, the more I recognized my traumatic Juncture as Favourable. I change my mind, changed my perception of the traumatic event, and change living in my pound-of-dirt. Rather than considering it my muck and mire, I used it to create a path for Exploring the Iceberg.

How did this happen?

There have been many Turning Points in my life and more Choice Points. Yet for me, there have been three significant Choice Points after my traumatic Turning Point – the car crash.

The first significant Choice Point I made was in my Near Death Experience. Rather than stay where I was in my NDE, I chose and asked to come back. That was the Favourable Juncture. I am here to do what I believe I am here to do, right now. This Choice Point led to my second.

The second significant Choice Point was to accept and welcome the trauma. My growth progressed exponentially. This encouraged me to change my mind. My trauma became treasure. As mentioned, rather than sink into my pound-of-dirt, I used my dirt to build my path to journey.

The third Choice Point emerged from the first two. Because I discovered my trauma was treasure it welcomed me to reinvent and rebuild myself into who I am and where I am today using my Iceberg Strategies. I learned through the Strategies how to emerge my self-esteem and the Strategies emerged the beginning of my self-esteem without instigation.

That's what the Strategies can do. They can be there for you even without calling on them. Ingraining the Iceberg Strategies they become inherent in you and, initially, blossom without nurture.

I asked myself different questions – as described in Part IV Chapter Six – Thinking and Language. My thoughts went from 'why did this happen to me?' to 'what can I do with what happened to me?'. To emphasize an undercurrent to the book – Changing my thinking changed my behaviour.

Needing Favourable Junctures in life is concomitant to making them visible.

Favourable Junctures became visible when I needed them. I began to Explore the Iceberg in a purposeful and meaningful way. I learned of me more deeply and clearly. That was when God and the universe conspired to help me to begin seeing with truthful eyes. This set me free. Not only was I given a treasure from the trauma, Favourable Junctures became visible fro me to get things accomplished and move forward into my primary and secondary reasons for being here. Only when I chose my trauma as treasure, did my life spiral down into the Iceberg.

I am Exploring the Iceberg currently and will continue for the rest of my life. I will always live the book. I am thriving and seeing the Favourable Junctures that are visible at my current level of self-awareness.

You are invited to Strive to Thrive. I urgently invite you to use the Iceberg Strategies. Explore the Iceberg. Strengthen your truthful eyes to live with passion in a less burdensome and more abundant life. This will procure the truth and set you free.

PRLs of Wisdom*

You are already Exploring the Iceberg …

GLOSSARY

- **80/20 Rule**: The percentage of time and/or work on moving forward (80 percent), and remaining stagnant or moving backwards (20 percent) – often used in conjunction with the Venting Valve.

- **Appropriate responsibility**: Refers to character. Character that has integrity is forthright, and genuine, even when no one is watching. 'Appropriateness' aligns with stages of life (a three year old has different responsibilities than a 21 year-old)

- **Briggs, Isabel Myers**: Creator and developer of the Myers-Briggs Type Indicator (MBTI) providing the 'constructive use of differences' from the work of Carl Gustav Jung.

- **Briggs, Catherine**: daughter of Isabel Myers Briggs and co-developer of the MBTI.

- **Carl Gustav Jung**: (1875-1961), M.D., assistant staff physician, mental clinic in Zurich, lecturer in psychiatry University of Zurich, worked closely with Sigmund Freud. Published Psychological Types (1921), Archetypes and the Collective Unconscious, Psychology and Alchemy.

- **Circle Vision Attitude:** What is good for me is good for you and what is good for you is good for me.

- **Continuum (see also Dimensions)**: The 4 extreme opposite preference pairs or aspects of human personality are described on 4 Continuums (E/I. S/N, T/F, J/P). Between the polar opposite preferences are not fixed but on a sliding scale or continuum.

- *Dimensions* (see also Continuum): The 4 extreme opposite preference pairs or aspects of human personality are described as 4 Continuums (E/I. S/N, T/F, J/P).

- *Favourable Junctures:* Invisible opportunities and possibilities waiting to be made visible by you increasing depth of self-awareness.

- *MBTI*: Myers-Briggs Type Indicator enduring since 1942 and accepted in 1962 in the psychological academics. It is the most sought after indicator in the world to determine a person's Jungian type.

- *Organizations*: Refers to a voluntary or paid workplace, business, industry or family.

- *Pound-of-dirt*: The measure of nastiness that occurs throughout life. Everyone eats a pound-of-dirt before they die.

- *Preferences*: Four categories that describe each type, defining different life preferences - Extrovert/Introvert, Sensing/iNtuition, Thinking/Feeling, Judging/Perceiving

- *Synergistic Enhancement*: Win-learn links with Synergistic Enhancement. Greater than the sum of its parts. Each unit influencing another unit in a spiralling upward climb moving forward and beyond.

- ***Transactional Analysis***: social psychology developed by Eric Berne, MD. TA is a tool that eliminates dysfunctional behaviour and reinforces healthy functioning (see, e.g. the books - 'I'm OK, You're OK' or 'Games People Play').

- ***Venting Valve***: An Iceberg Strategy used when exasperation, complaints, frustration, sadness, loneliness and other like notions need to be expressed using the 80/20 Rule.

PRLs of Wisdom*

George Eliot said:

"It's never too late to be what you might have been."

Appendix I

Acquired Brain Injury

THE STORY OF ...
ACQUIRED BRAIN INJURY

Acquired Brain Injury (ABI) is an injury to the brain from outside trauma, stroke or heart attack. It is called Acquired because it occurred after birth. Brain injury is unpredictable in its consequences. Brain injury effects who we are, the way we think, act, and feel. It can change everything about a person in a matter of seconds.

Overview of Traumatic Brain Injury

My ABI is classified as a *Traumatic* brain injury (TBI) and can significantly affect many cognitive, physical, and psychological skills. Physical deficit can include ambulation, balance, co-ordination, fine motor skills, strength, and endurance. Cognitive deficits of language and communication, information processing, memory, and perceptual skills are common. Psychological status is also often altered.

The Glasgow Coma Scale measures the severity of a coma including:

- Alertness

- Verbal Stimulus Response

- Painful Stimulus Response

- Unresponsive

A feature of a severe brain injury is a prolonged unconscious state or coma lasts days, weeks, or months.

Closed Head Injury

With a closed head injury, when the brain swells, haemorrhaging inside the skull has no place to expand, as the scalp does not recede to accommodate the swelling. This can cause an increase in intracranial pressure the brain can expand through any available opening in the skull, including the eye sockets. When the brain expands through the eye sockets, it can compress and impair the functions of the eye nerves. My left eye was pushed out of its eye socket. This can cause brain tissues to compress, causing further injury.

Neurons and nerve tracts can be affected, disabling any messages that tell the brain what to do. This results in changes to:

- Thinking

- Physical abilities

- Personality

- Behavioural abilities

These changes are on a continuum from temporary to permanent. Some possible changes as a result of any brain injury are described below.

Thinking Changes	Physical Changes	Personality and Behavioural Changes
• Decision making • Planning • Sequencing • Judgment • Attention • Communication • Reading and writing skills • Thought processing speed • Problem solving skills • Organization • Self-perception • Perception • Thought flexibility • Safety awareness • New learning	• Muscle movement • Muscle co-ordination • Sleep • Hearing • Vision • Taste • Smell • Touch • Fatigue • Weakness • Balance • Speech • Seizures • Sexual functioning	• Social skills • Emotional control and mood swings • Appropriateness of behaviour • Reduced self-esteem • Depression • Anxiety • Frustration • Stress • Denial • Self-centeredness • Anger management • Coping skills • Self-monitoring remarks or actions • Motivation • Irritability or agitation • Excessive laughing or crying

There is no cure for an ABI. There is time, patience, and acceptance of the symptoms of the injury and acceptance of life. Recovery can be dramatic in the beginning then slow right down to a crawl after the first few months. My complete recovery will never be. The old Paul is gone and a new Paul was born post trauma coming out of a coma.

Appendix II

THE NEVER ENDING STORY

THE NEVER ENDING STORY

I was finally discharged from the West Cottage. My assessments became a never-ending story. I spent another month in a hospital in Toronto followed by six or seven more months at home.

At home there were more new friends, outreach therapists with the Acquired Brain Injury Community Services.

I have a very thin memory of this time. I asked my Vocational Therapist at the time, Justine Best, to write this chapter.

Justine Best

Community Intervention Coordinator

An Acquired Brain Injury Program

Paul returned home to be with his family and thought: back to reality of his life prior to the accident. The truth: Paul is different and so is his life. He is no longer the individual who wakes up early each morning to go for a long distance run or the father who had the ability to focus on the lives of his children, or the enthusiastic consultant and teacher for the ministry of correctional services. He now struggles each morning with fatigue and with his inability to remember the things he needs to do for himself. These struggles make it difficult to focus on his children and his extremely low energy levels make it difficult to even think of working full-time. He wanted so desperately to return to his old life but was unable to plan how to do it or physically able to participate at the level he once did.

Our program received a referral for Paul to initiate a Community Re-entry and Vocational Re-entry Plan. I was assigned to his case. Paul requested that I write this section of his book due to his difficulty remembering details of this time.

Paul identified his goals as: return to work, return to driving and to become a part of his children's life once again. The first item on the agenda was to develop a return to work plan, not withstanding his desire to focus on his children. We initially arranged a visit to his work site. This was not where Paul wanted to begin. He did not want a therapist with him and thought he should be able to work up to a full-time day within a week's time. He did not envision a plan that would involve several months.

Following the first visit to the work site Paul became aware of the reasons why it was so important to develop a plan, however, he continued to want to do it his way. His way was "all or nothing" and we had many long discussions as to why this was not possible. His mood began to reflect his frustrations and his inability to perform like the old Paul. We spent many hours discussing how the old Paul had different capabilities and why we must focus on the new Paul and his needs. Again this was not an idea that Paul was prepared to accept. Paul did agree, however, to counselling and began attending sessions on weekly basis. This definitely did not solve all the problems but it was a start.

Paul continued to focus on his return to work and agreed to follow the plan we developed. In the initial design, Paul would attend work for two hours, three times per week and increased his hours as was appropriate and manageable. In the beginning, we spent time orienting Paul to his office and the systems he followed prior to the trauma. Paul's reluctances to implement new strategies into his office space and work, made it difficult to get started. At this point we began to initiate meetings with his supervisor to discuss Paul's new role in the work place. The supervisor assigned Paul to teaching classes to Probation Officers at his workplace. He found this frustrating; he felt he had been demoted. Prior to the accident, Paul focused on innovative topics and methods of teaching. Previously, Paul's teaching skills were well recognized and he had made many guest appearances at province wide conferences and workshops. Thus it was hard for him to change his methods, but eventually Paul agreed to start teaching adults in the classroom as the beginning step.

Paul's natural teaching skills were still strong, however, evidence of some of the cognitive changes began to challenge his ability. This again frustrated Paul. We discussed strategies that could be implemented and his teaching skills improved over time.

Paul took on new and progressive challenges over time and eventually found his way back into a position he enjoyed. As his therapist I began to fade my involvement to enable Paul to experience his work responsibilities more independently. Paul and I organized this fading process according to how he felt about his capacities. The process moved faster than I felt comfortable with but Paul always remained strong and conquered his own issues with his own strategies. There were times when Paul would call and request some assistance but these were few and far between. Intervention for Paul formally finished in 1999. Today Paul continues to struggle with fatigue and is unable to work a full day, however, he continues with his professional career and finds his work meaningful.

In addition to the return to work process, Paul also struggled with many things in his personal life. His marriage dissolved, the family home was sold, and his children became more independent. This along with the work challenges impacted Paul's mood to the point that his therapist and family were extremely concerned that Paul may be at risk from an emotional perspective. Paul's attitude towards his recovery, the ongoing love and support from his family, counselling, and a renewed zest for life all contributed to his ability to conquer the challenges arising from the initial injury.

Prior to the accident Paul competed in trail running races. His left hemiparsis caused weakness in his entire left side and a change in his gait. Paul and I began a walking program with the goal to run. Paul recognized his running gait looked awkward and to him it felt sloppy. Paul also wished to return to running the trails. He refused to run on the street in case someone saw him. He could no longer run on the wooded trails due to the many obstacles. He eventually agreed to run on trails that were flat with few obstacles. Paul wanted to continue work on running on his own, and I knew he had accomplished this goal when he requested that I enter a 5km race with him. Paul completed the race.

In this entire process Paul began to adjust to the "new" Paul and has become comfortable with who he is today. He offers new skills to his family, workplace and society that are fulfilling to all. To this therapist I consider this to be one of the most successful community re-entry programs. I attribute this success to Paul's attitude and ability to accept the "new" Paul. This is when his recovery soared to success.

Appendix III

Corporate and Family

PREAMBLE

This book is about personal, professional and organizational growth. At the beginning of the book you were invited to shape your definition of the word "organization". Throughout the book I have stated or implied the growing similarities of individuals and organizations. The following chapter is a strong piece, kindly provided by its author, merging the notion of both individuals and family with organizations. It continues to merge theory and practice. This previously unpublished article provides personal experience from the author Pamela Hill, as well as social and cultural scenarios.

COMPARING FAMILY VALUES TO THE CHARACTER OF ORGANIZATIONS

Unpublished work printed with permission
Pamela Hill, Eastern Michigan University

ABSTRACT

The workforce of 2000 is increasingly becoming the family of 2000. As we spend more time with our jobs and careers and less time with our biological families, the dynamics of the workplace has taken on the appearance of a family system. Whatever habits, traits, values, or joys are part of our makeup, they exhibit themselves in our organizations. These habits, traits, value and joys of individuals within organizations become integrated into the core character of an organization. When we examine gender differences, we find that as women expand their roles within organizations, nurturing and a sense of shared success becomes part of the organization's character.

INTRODUCTION

66 *W*hat lies behind us and what lies before us are tiny matters compared to what lies within us". These words spoken by Ralph Waldo Emerson quietly reflect the very essence of our identity. Mr. Emerson is not here for me to interview, but my own belief is that he was referring to our character and value systems. When you take this quote and apply it to organizations, character becomes a life issue, not simply one of work. My motivation in approaching the topic of character in organizations and gender differences comes from my own professional experience and as the mother of five children. As a manger and mother, the roles I play are often interchangeable. I find that my values in both roles are consistent with how I view myself as mentor, caregiver, and teacher. In turn, this congruence within roles defines my character and values to those around me, whether it is my teen-age son, a colleague or manager. In the absence of congruence, the family systems, both personal and professional will suffer. The body of this paper will focus on organizations as families. I see no better way to define character and the impact it has on organizations than to view organizations as families.

ORGANIZATION AS FAMILY

The cliché "we are a product of our environment", is perhaps more telling now than ever before. Dr. Stewart Tubbs, author of The Systems Approach to Small Group Interactions, states: "Primary groups usually include one's family and closest friends. Certainly the vast majority of attitudes and values people hold are a result of the influence of their primary groups. Primary groups influence self-concept as well as personality from childhood to adulthood. (Tubbs, p107).

As infants, our primary group consists of those who assume the role of caregiver. This group can include biological parents, siblings, medical professionals or strangers. As one grows and matures, the values and ethics reflected by the primary group influence the development of character in the individual. Self-image comes from experiences growing up within these primary groups. But it is not the experiences that determine who we are; it is our responses to these experiences. We've all heard stories of individuals who have overcome hardships and tragedies during their formative years and as adults, yet continue on their paths with a positive outlook and true caring for others. How does one thrive in the face of adversity? What sets these individuals apart? Senge uses the term "personal mastery" in identifying these individuals. This personal mastery embodies two underlying movements. The first one of clarifying what is important and second, continually learning how to see current reality more clearly. (Senge, p141).

These individuals adapt and find creative solutions to problems. They continue throughout their lives to seek more information, more experiences and more joy in their lives. It is this continual quest for information that takes these individuals to the helm of organizations.

It is difficult to discuss organizations as families without first determining the roles that managers, leaders and the workers play. Examining leadership traits, I am struck by how parental this role is. As mother or father figures, leaders set the tone for the organization. These leaders draw from their past professional experiences to make decisions and move organizations. These leaders also draw, sometimes subconsciously, from their family history. Their style and value systems can mimic the same kind of communication and responses in an organization that is played out in their family units. Parents and leaders who possess a strong sense of caring and nurturing can eventually step aside and observe their positive influences on their children and employees. These parents and leaders receive their greatest satisfaction from the successes of others.

In order for someone to have true greatness, there must lie within them the ability to recognize greatness in those around them. As a manager and as a parent, I find myself relating to my employees and children in a similar fashion. Applauding successes, allowing mistakes and listening with interest all are part of the nurturing environment needed to grow and develop.

In approaching the growth and development of children and workers, I would be remiss in not addressing the influence children or workers have on one another. In healthy family systems, siblings are first and foremost the focus of parenting. Children may feel that there are inequities within the family in regards to recognition and rewards. Parents who listen closely and respond in a timely manner can minimize these feelings of inequities and assist the child with increasing their self-awareness. The same is true for leaders in organizations. Leaders who listen to workers will have more success in the workplace than those who are busy listening to themselves. Communication in both family and professional settings is very difficult when everyone is talking and no one is listening. When families are part of group therapy, the first thing that occurs is listening. In order to problem solve, the problem must be heard. Sometimes simply being heard solves a large part of the problem. Organizational consultants go into organizations as another pair of ears. They listen to the workers and the leaders much the same as a family therapist does in a family therapy setting. In his textbook, Psychology in Industrial Organizations, Maier theorizes that allowing the workers to express feelings leads to clarification on issues and brings about a change in the feelings and attitudes associated with them. This same conclusion has been found in family therapy settings. Once the communication door is opened, the task of healing and growing can begin.

The issue of control within families and organizations cannot be overlooked. Control within these systems can take many forms. Withholding, commanding, intimidating and manipulating can all be considered methods of control, as can problem solving, mentoring, sharing and rewarding.

One example of control issues within organizations is the role that unions have. Unions play a big part in control of some organizations.

Unions came about because the "parental figures" within companies were abusing their "children". The unions became the social workers, that is, they were not part of the immediate family, but were called in to mediate and advocate for those not in control. But, unions can also create a concern among the workers. How much control should a union have? Does it always do what is in the best interest of the workers? And as within family systems, do the social workers (unions) make mistakes? All of these questions point to situations similar to what families may face.

THE THIRD FAMILY

Families, organizations, schools and communities are becoming integrated into what can best be described as the "third" family. Programs, which focus on self-esteem, character, values and feelings, are becoming part of our educational system. The common thread is the goal of raising the level of social and emotional competence in children as a part of their regular educational system. The common thread is the goal of raising the level of social and emotional competence in children as a part of their regular education (Goldman, p280). Goleman notes that developing the ability to set aside one's self centred focus has social benefit, opening the way for empathy and real listening which can lead to greater caring and compassion (Goldman, p285). But these are not lessons to be taught. Every action in our lives teaches those around us about morals and defines our character. "Do as I say, not as I do" (anon) speaks to the damage done to our future leaders by those who are not congruent with the values and ethics they dictate.

"Psychoethis", a term coined by Terri Kaye Needle and Martin J. Lecker, may best describe how psychological makeup guides ethical decision making (Needle and Lecker, p32). Their research draws upon numerous psychological theories to define this new discipline. One of the case studies reviewed in their work was on Anita Roddick, owner of Body Shop. Ms. Roddick began her business in the mid 1970's in cosmetic products. She quickly gained attention for her truth in advertising of her products. As her business flourished, she expanded her social consciousness by joining Green Peace and supporting the cause by advertising in her shops. Ms. Roddick used her success to promote her social concerns. Linking her business success with her social values provides a positive model for leadership. The Golden Rule can only be the Golden Rule when it is practiced and not quoted as a value statement for families or organizations.

GENDER AND CHARACTER

The increased number of women in the workforce has had a tremendous impact on the values of the workplace. This has caused employees and organizations to re-evaluate their self-concept. Women tend to be more open with personalizing the workplace. This openness has also led to greater awareness of the kind of family values that the workplace may embody.

Female leaders exhibit certain characteristics different from those of male leaders. Some of the early roles females had in organizations were those of support and human relations. This seemed a natural match with the nurturing and protecting traits that females possess. In most cultures, women have been socialized to fulfill these roles with their families and friends. When these same women began entering the workforce in large numbers and moving up the ranks in management, they found that the traditional male management model was one of control and setting limits. Women saw opportunities for change and empowerment. When this change was attempted, women experienced some of the same discrimination that faced blacks in the 1960's. Women were leaving their "traditional" roles as sisters, mothers and daughters and stepping into their father's role. Although women were leaving their traditional roles, they did not leave their communication style at home. Fortunately, there has been some movement in the business world to adopt a more feminine style of management. In their book Megatrends for Women, Pat Aburdene and John Naisbitt assert that: "Primitive descriptions of the "manager of the future" uncannily match those of female leadership. Consultants try to teach male managers to relinquish the command-and-control mode. For women it was different: it just came naturally" (Aburdene and Naisbitt, p88).

The feminine style of leadership really began emerging as the United States moved from the industrial age into the information age. The information age has forced upon our organizations the need to change and adapt quickly. Women managers, with little background in military structure or sports, could not relate well to these masculine metaphors used in business. So women relied on their instincts to lead and create within their organizations.

The information age demands a multi-task approach to work. What better way to accomplish tasks than to have a mother leading and empowering workers to meet deadlines?

Empowerment is one of the most visible attributes in a feminine leadership style. Allowing others to have some control and input into decisions creates an atmosphere of shared expectations. This is much like the way a mother helps her child learn to walk. She encourages, and allows the child to fall, all the time protecting the child by remaining close at hand for any real dangers. The child takes his first steps and looks to his mother for continued encouragement. As he takes more steps, he becomes more self-confident and moves faster without looking to mother as much. The greatest satisfaction a mother can have is to watch the child cross the room alone. By letting go, she has empowered the child to succeed.

Nurturing and caring are other attributes that are considered feminine characteristics but are often confused in the workplace as weakness and being soft. Mothers nurture and care for their children while balancing the need to be firm and objective when necessary. Being a nice leader does not mean that hard decisions can't be made when required. That is too often the perception that workers have of female leaders. If they are nice, they can't cut the hard stuff. If they are objective managers, they are considered difficult people. This again, goes to the mother as manger role. Female managers must do both;

be supportive of their workers and lead the organization forward to success

Being a mother has been a great teacher for me. When your first child is born, you immediately begin wearing many hats: teacher, role model, friend, mentor and helper. I discovered an important book after the birth of my daughter: My Mother, My Self by Nancy Friday. I was investigating all the possible information I could to raise my daughter with a heightened sense of self. The book provided me with numerous examples of mother-daughter relationships and how these roles affect women in professional settings. Ms. Friday's book speaks at length about the need for women to establish their own support systems beyond their parents.

These feminine traits are not exclusive to females. As more women have joined the ranks of management or become business owners, there has been more recognition of these successes by male leaders. When reviewing the characteristics of successful male leaders, we find that many of them possess some of the same characteristics as the successful female mangers.

If we examine environment as one indicator of defining feminine and masculine characteristics, we find that childhood development plays a large part in leadership styles. Cultural expectations are based on gender differences and are a determining factor for individual experiences. Boys are expected to "do" while girls are encouraged to "be".

Girls are encouraged to relate closely to mothers while boys are reminded of the differences between males and females. While the physical differences are the most obvious, differences in character and behaviour are the outcome of these cultural expectations. Conversely, gender-blind environments that promote discovery and self-awareness along with caring and compassion can provide a basis for leadership styles that also promote consistent values. Male and female leadership styles can be based on the same mode. Encouraging our children to first explore and define their own values is the first step in creating organizations based on shared expectations, and not on biased thinking and control.

Integrating personal values into the workplace can be difficult when the language used is not consistent. Male and female differences in communication styles can undermine even the most sincere attempt at organizational change. These style differences can begin at the worker's desk or front line and continue to the boardroom. Caring leaders will find a way to present information to the audience in a manner that is understood and non-threatening. Even if the message the leader has to deliver is negative, how it is presented will have a bigger impact on how it is received than the actual information. When we view ourselves as parents communicating with our children, we allow more of our compassion and feelings to guide our words.

Women tend to put themselves at the centre of their organizations rather than at the top, thus emphasizing both accessibility and equality, and that they laboured constantly to include people in their decision-making (Helgesen, p10). Helgesen continues to describe the female communication and leadership style as a "web of inclusion" (Helgesen, p10). This web of inclusion mimics a healthy family system by placing the leader or parental figure at the centre of the organization or family.

In times of crisis, pulling together as a family unit can bring added benefits to an organization. Sharing the wealth as well as the crisis gives ownership to the workers. Parents who provide their children with constant input find that when a family crisis occurs, these same children respond by offering to help and may even have a more objective view of the situation than the parents do.

Children and workers that are valued gain a sense of value about themselves and regard those around them as adding value to their life. Children and workers who are not provided information and are not valued will view themselves as helpless and in turn, will become helpless. Leading a family or organization through a crisis can be considered a test of character for some. The true test comes from continuing to lead after the crisis.

An organization as an organism is perhaps the best way of looking at the changes in leadership style. Organizations that work the way life does are more congenial environments for human beings to exist in (Helgesen, p16). With this existence comes the desire to thrive and grow. Building organizations, which allow this growth, will be the key to America's global successes in the year 2000.

CONCLUSION

Defining character within an organization is a difficult task. Applying a family systems approach to initiate change in organizations can simplify even the most complex organizational structure. Organizations are made up of groups of people with different values and personalities. And although families are comprised of biological members and may outwardly exhibit a consistent character, upon close examination, it is found that each individual family member has differences in both personality and values. These differences come from gender, age and life experiences. It is the blending of organizational and family systems that is important if we are to continue to succeed and thrive. The face of America's workplace is changing. On-site day care, health clubs, spousal support groups, and family leave benefits have led the way for the integration of family values into the workplace.

Combining organizational requirements with family needs is a reality if we are to continue to compete globally as a nation. To meet theses needs, we must create more interdisciplinary programs in our schools and universities and provide closer linkages to our communities and businesses. Preparing children for adulthood does not begin with college. It is crucial that we provide self-awareness and mentoring programs during the formative years. If we do not learn, we do not grow. If we do not grow, we risk losing ourselves in mediocrity.

Paul Lamb

REFERENCES

Paul Lamb

REFERENCES

Aburdene, Patricia and Naisbitt, John. Megatrends for Women. New York: Random House, 1992.

Canefield, Jack and Miller, Jacqueline. Heart at Work. New York: McGraw-Hill; 1996.

Friday, Nancy. My Mother, My Self. New York: Dell Publishing; 1977.

Goleman, Daniel. Emotional Intelligence. New York: Bantam Books; 1995.

Helgesen, Sally. The Web of Inclusion. New York: Currency Doubleday; 1995.

Hill, Pamela. Original quote. Ann Arbor; 1997.

Maier, Norman R. F. and Berser, Gertrude Casselman. Psychology in Industrial Organizations. Boston: Houghton Mifflin Co.: 1982

Needle, Terri Kaye and Lecker, Martin J. "Psychoethics: A Discipline Applying Psychology to Ethics. Review of Business, St John's University: 1997, Vol 18, p 30-34.

Senge, Peter M. The Fifth Discipline. New York: Currency Doubleday, 1990.

Tigner, Steven S. "Souls in Conflict." Journal for A Just and Caring Education, 1996, Vol 2 p 349-359.

Tubbs, Stewart L. A Systems Approach to Small group Interaction. New York: McGraw-Hill, Inc; 1992.

Appendix IV

STRENGTHS
KNOWING
TYPE

STRENGTHS KNOWING TYPE

Strengths and wisdom can be enhanced by knowing your Myers-Briggs Type Indicator. It can fully contribute to:

- Enhancing communication

- Understanding others

- Enhancing the organization

- Working better together

- Leadership

- Enhanced meetings/group work

- Enhancing choices for you and the organization

- Making more informed decisions

- Doing what you are

- Creating less stress

- Enhancing coping skills

- Exploring the Iceberg

Appendix V

MYERS-BRIGGS
TYPE INDICATOR

THE MYERS-BRIGGS TYPE INDICATOR (MBTI)

What Is Type?

Type was created by Carl Gustav Jung and made understandable by Myers and Briggs. The following charts describe the preferences in more detail.

How to read the charts:

Box One: describes to what the preference refers.

Box Two: with two columns, one for each preference: describes in point form the preference characteristics and is aligned with its opposite preference

(e.g. E aligned with I)

EXTROVERT/INTROVERT—From where we get Energy

The Extrovert and Introvert (E/I) This dimension describes from where we prefer to get our energy – how do we get energized when exhausted. Some people are mostly energized outside themselves through other people or things – Extroverting. Some people are mostly energized inside themselves – Introverting. Although we have both we prefer to use one more than the other.

Extrovert	Introvert
The Afterthinkers	The Forethinkers
• Sociable	• Territorial
• Interactive	• Concentrative
• Breadth of interest	• Intensive
• Multiple relationships	• Limited relationships
• Gregarious	• Reflective
• Expend energy	• Conserve energy
• Cannot understand life until they have lived it	• Cannot live life until they understand it
• Attitude relaxed and confident. They expect the water to prove shallow, and plunge readily into new and untried experiences	• Attitude reserved and questioning. They expect the waters to prove deep, and pause to take soundings in the new and untried
• Minds outwardly directed, interest and attention following objective happenings, primarily those of the immediate environment. Their real world therefore is the outer world of people and things	• Minds inwardly directed, frequently unaware of the objective environment, interest and attention being engrossed by inner events. Their real world therefore is the inner world of ideas and understanding

• The civilizing genius, the people of action and practical achievement, who go from doing to considering and back to doing	• The cultural genius, the people of ideas and abstract invention, who go from considering to doing and back to considering
• Conduct in essential matters is always governed by objective conditions	• Conduct in essential matters is always governed by subjective values.
• Spend themselves lavishly upon external claims and conditions which to them constitute life	• Defend themselves as far as possible against external claims and conditions in favour of the inner life
• Understandable and accessible, often sociable, more at home in the world of people and things than in the world of ideas	• Subtle and impenetrable, often taciturn and shy, more at home in the world of ideas than in the world of people and things
• Expansive and less impassioned, they unload their emotions as they go along	• Intense and passionate, they bottle up their emotions and guard them carefully as high explosives
• Typical weakness lies in a tendency toward intellectual superficiality, very conspicuous in extreme types	• Typical weakness lies in a tendency toward impracticality, very conspicuous in extreme types
• Health and wholesomeness depend upon a reasonable development of balancing introversion	• Health and wholesomeness depend upon a reasonable development of balancing extraversion

SENSING/INTUITION – To what we **attend**

The Sensing and Intuition (S/N) This dimension describes to what we prefer to pay attention. Some people mostly pay attention to details in the here and now – Sensing. Some people mostly pay attention to the big picture and are future oriented – iNtuitives. The letter 'N' is used here as the letter 'I' is used previously with Introvert. Although we have both we prefer to use one more than the other.

Sensors	i**N**tuitives
• Sequential	• Random
• Present	• Future-oriented
• Realistic	• Fantasize
• Actual	• Potential
• Down-to-earth	• Head-in-the-clouds
• Factual	• Possibilities
• Practical	• Impracticality
• Specific	• General
• Present	• Future-oriented
• Face life observantly, craving enjoyment	• Face life expectantly, craving inspiration
• Observant at the expense of imagination	• Imaginative at the expense of observation.
• Are by nature pleasure lovers and consumers; loving life as it is and having a great capacity for enjoyment, they are in general contented	• Are by nature initiators, inventors and promoters; having no taste for life as it is, and small capacity for living in and enjoying the present, they are generally restless

• Desiring chiefly to possess and enjoy, and being very observant, they are imitative, wanting to have what other people have and to do what other people do, and are very dependent upon their physical surroundings	• Desiring chiefly opportunities and possibilities, and being very imaginative, they are inventive and original, quite indifferent to what other people have and do, and are very independent of their physical surroundings
• Dislike intensely any and every occupation which requires the suppression of sensing, and are most reluctant to sacrifice present enjoyment to future gain or good.	• Dislike intensely any and every occupation which necessitates sustained concentration on sensing, and are willing to sacrifice the present to a large extent since they neither live in it nor particularly enjoy it
• Contribute to the public welfare by their support of every form of enjoyment, recreation, and every variety of comfort, luxury, and beauty	• Contribute to the public welfare by their inventiveness, initiative, enterprise, and powers of inspired leadership in every direction of human interest
• Are always in danger of being frivolous, unless balance is attained through development of intuition	• Are always in danger of being fickle, changeable, and lacking in persistence, unless balance is attained through development of a judging process

THINKING/FEELING – How we make **decisions**

The Thinking and Feeling (T/F) This dimension describes how we prefer to make decisions or come to conclusion. Some people mostly make decisions through critical evaluation, logic, objectivity, laws or policies, firmness – Thinkers. Some people mostly make decisions through values, harmony – Feelers. Although we have both we prefer to use one than the other.

Thinkers	Feelers
• Thinkers make decisions through logic - if this, then that. Thinkers are objective, firm, just and critique	• Feelers make decisions that are subjective, need harmony and are based on values.
• Detached	• Appreciative
• Value logic above sentiment.	• Value sentiment above logic
• Usually impersonal, being more interested in things than in relationships	• Usually personal, being more interested in people than in things
• If forced to choose between truthfulness and tactfulness will usually be truthful	• If forced to choose between tactfulness and truthfulness will usually be tactful.
• Stronger in executive ability than in the social arts	• Stronger in the social arts than in executive ability
• Are likely to question the conclusions of other people on principle-believing them probably wrong	• Are likely to agree with those around them, thinking as other people think, believing them probably right

Paul Lamb

• Naturally brief and businesslike, they often seem to lack friendliness and sociability without knowing or intending it	• Naturally friendly, whether sociable or not, they find it difficult to be brief and businesslike
• Are usually able to organize facts and ideas into a logical sequence that states the subject, makes the necessary points. Comes to a conclusion and stops there without repetition	• Usually find it hard to know where to start a statement or in what order to present what they have to say. May therefore ramble and repeat themselves, with more detail than a thinker wants or thinks necessary
• Contribute to the welfare of society by the intellectual criticism of its habits, customs, and beliefs, by the exposure of wrongs, the solution of problems, and the support of science and research for the enlargement of human knowledge and understanding	• Contribute to the welfare of society by their loyal support of good works and those movements, generally regarded as good by the community, which they feel correctly about and so can serve effectively
• More often men than women, and when married to a feeling type naturally become guardian of the spouse's neglected and unreliable thinking	• More often women than men, and when married to a thinker frequently become guardian of the partner's sometimes neglected and harassed feelings

JUDGING/PERCEIVING – How we **act** in the world

The Judging and Perceiving (J/P) Continuum describes how we are in the world. Some people are mostly planned, time oriented and scheduled with being organized as a core preference – Judging. Some people mostly are mostly flexible, spontaneous and adaptable – Perceivers. Although we have both we prefer to use one than the other.

Judging	**P**erceiving
• More decisive than curious	• More curious than decisive
• Live according to plans, standards, and customs not easily or lightly set aside, to which the situation of the moment must, if possible, be made to conform	• Live according to the situation of the moment and adjust themselves easily to the accidental and the unexpected
• Make a very definite choice among life's possibilities, but may not appreciate or utilize unplanned, unexpected, and incidental happenings	• Frequently masterful in their handling of the unplanned, unexpected, and incidental, but may not make an effective choice among life's possibilities
• Rational -- depend upon reasoned judgements, their own or borrowed from someone else, to protect them from unnecessary or undesirable experiences.	• Empirical, they depend on their readiness for anything and everything to bring them a constant flow of new experience--much more than they can digest or use

• Like to have matters settled and decided as promptly as possible, so that they will know what is going to happen and can plan for it and be prepared for it	• Like to keep decisions open as long as possible before doing anything irrevocable, because they don't know nearly enough about it yet
• Think or feel that they know what other people ought to do about almost everything, and are not averse to telling them	• Know what other people are doing, and are interested to see how it comes out
• Take real pleasure in getting something finished, out of the way, and off their minds	• Take great pleasure in starting something new, until the newness wears off
• Inclined to regard the Perceptive types as aimless drifters	• Inclined to regard the Judging types as only half-alive
• Aim to be right	• Aim to miss nothing
• Self-regimented, exacting	• Flexible, adaptable, and tolerant

Adapted from:

1. Myers, Isabel Briggs, McCaulley, Mary H., Quenk, Noami L., Hammer, Allen L., MBTI Manual: A Guide to the Development and Use of the Myers-Briggs Type Indicator, Third Addition, 1998.

2. Isabel Briggs Myers, with Peter Myers Gifts Differing, 1989.

COMMUNICATION AND LANGUAGE
THROUGH CARL JUNG AND MYERS-BRIGGS

Communication is in the top three issues that need attending in both personal and organizational life. Communication is how we get along. One hundred percent of our communication is done:

- **Verbally** – *what* we say

- **Tone** – *how* we say it

- **Body language** – *entire body* including (arms, hand, fingers, legs, feet...) and face (mouth, forehead, hair, eyes...)

Personality Types communicate in type no matter the worldly language spoken. We have more of an opportunity to get what we want attending to the other's language!

How often have you said to another, 'Were you listening?'; 'Were you paying attention?'

Speaking the other's language helps them pay attention and listen. Speaking the other's language puts a mirror up and they see someone similar. In other words, the other person's ears perk up and there is a better chance of their paying attention to you and what you are saying. Therefore, the other person understands in a clear manner leading to a better chance of getting what you want cooperatively.

The following charts describe how each preference communicates. In conversations with these types of preferences, the charts provide the words or language you could use with these types of people. This will increase the likelihood of getting what you want, or at least communicating clearly.

E/I – Preferred Response	
EXTROVERT Some people prefer to: Talk It Out	**I**NTROVERT Some people prefer to: Think It Through
How to communicate with:	How to communicate with:
a. Ask open ended questions	a. Pre-alert the person with an agenda or memo
b. Allow enough time	b. Possibly plan to meet twice; first to outline the task or issues; second, to consider proposed solutions
c. Keep the person on topic	c. Brainstorm on paper first, then ask for verbal responses
Extroverts prefer to: • Speak, listen, speak, speak, listen, speak, speak, speak – then perhaps reflect • Talk: Talk things out with energy and enthusiasm • Expect a quick response • Prefer talking with groups • Prefer face-to-face rather than written or voicemail over email • In groups or meetings, may talk aloud to create ideas for discussion	Introverts prefer to: • Listen, reflect, listen, reflect, reflect, reflect – then perhaps speak • Talk: by thinking things through, with energy and enthusiasm reserved • Expect a slow response, thinking things through • Prefer one-to-one or small familiar groups • Prefer written over face-to-face or email over voicemail • In groups or meetings, talk when ideas have been thought through

S/N – Preferred Response	
SENSING Some people prefer: Specifics	**IN**TUITION Some people prefer: Big Picture
How to communicate with:	How to communicate with:
a. Give the facts	a. Give the larger implications; how will it affect the bottom line, customer satisfaction, other areas, teams, etc?
b. Be concise	b. Talk about the effect of an error, not just what the error was
c. Have specific data to back up an idea or plan of action	c. Provide a context; relate ideas to each other
Sensing talks in facts and actualities	iNtuitive talks in theory and possibilities
• Pieces of the puzzle • Who? What? Where? When? • Talk: prefer to be presented first with facts, details, examples • Talking is orderly • Ideas need to be straightforward and feasible	• The whole puzzle • Big picture • Talk: prefer to be presented first with broad issues • Talking is roundabout • Prefers ideas to be novel

T/F – Preferred Response	
THINKING Some people prefer to hear: Logical Implications	**F**EELING Some prefer to focus on the: Impact On People
How to communicate with:	How to communicate with:
a. State objective reasons	a. Give results in terms of the impact on others
b. List the causes and effects	b. List the things that people care about
c. Focus on the "challenge of doing the work right"	c. Focus on the opportunity to be around people or to "make a difference"
Thinkers prefer: • Logical communication • Pros and cons of alternative • Detachment • Objectivity • To the point without emotions or rambling; how alternatives impact on organization • Critical and objective; impersonal reasoning • First present goals and objectives with feelings and then present emotions • Talk in organizational terms – organization first and foremost	Feelers prefer: • Values in communication • Attachment • Subjectivity • Personable and agreeable; how alternatives impact on people • Accepting and appreciative • First present points of agreement with goals and objectives secondarily • Talk in people terms – people first and foremost

J/P – Preferred Response	
JUDGING Some people prefer to: Come To Conclusion	**P**ERCEIVING Some people prefer to: Stay Open To Suggestions
How to communicate with:	How to communicate with:
a. Clarify what the goals are and when they should be reached	a. Consider or suggest some different approaches
b. Deliberately consider alternatives	b. Consider or suggest some sources of information
c. Stay open to possible solutions, prevent premature closure	c. Establish a time for a decision or action to be made
Judgers prefer:	Perceivers prefer:
• Communication with conclusion with decision • Goals, closure, timely • Timelines and scheduling • Prefers no surprises • Expect self to follow through as well as others • Decisions made as final • Groups or meetings focus on completing tasks	• Communicates in a spider-web with wait-and-see attitude • Open-ended, searching, flexible • Discussing timelines but avoids deadlines • Surprises OK • Expect others to respond to situational requirements • Decisions are tentative • Groups or meetings focus on process being used

COMMUNICATION TIPS

Tips are directed at each type as opposed to what to expect or hear from each type. Knowing how others see or what others hear acts on your noticing.

EXTROVERTS	**I**NTROVERTS
• Notice you may be overwhelming • Act more in silence. Perhaps saying: "It would be helpful to know where you stand on this issue we're discussing." Then be quiet and listen	• Notice you are responsible for letting people know where you are and what you need • Act by speaking up. Perhaps saying: "I want to participate in this, but I'm unsure about getting a word in. I'd like to step back and find a better process!"
SENSING	**I**NTUITIVES
• Give others the context for your details • Perhaps say: "I think this is a really good idea. Here are some of the pieces I may be able to help with...."	• Your ideas may need to be 'tried out' by looking at realities • Perhaps say: "What would make this idea work?"

THINKING	**F**EELING
• Notice your detachment and take action by using interpersonal connections and avoid sounding too critical, invite F's to participate in discussions and be patient with F's sensitivity and harmony which may be foreign to T's • Perhaps say: "How is the process working today?"	• Notice your attachment and taking critical sounding comments too personally. Speak in a logical and clear manner • Perhaps say: "I wonder if we can spend some time looking at the process we are using with the anger I'm feeling in the group?"
JUDGING	**P**ERCEIVING
• Notice you may appear too structure and restrictive	• Notice you may appear meandering and wasting time

Source:

Susan A. Brock, Ph.D, 1987

Adapted from Linda K. Kirby, 'Work Types'

Myers, Isabel Briggs, McCaulley, Mary H., Quenk, Noami L., Hammer, Allen L., MBTI Manual: A Guide to the Development and Use of the Myers-Briggs Type Indicator, Third Addition, 1998.

234

Appendix VI

INSPIRED READERS' TESTIMONIALS

Letter I Received After a TV Interview

September 5, 2000

Dear Paul

Everyday I meet interesting people but I must say your attitude and fighting spirit touched my heart. You truly are an amazing person.

Thank you for sharing your story with us and I'm glad to see there is a happy ending.

Sincerely,

Jee-Yun

PRLs OF WISDOM

Carl Gustav Jung said:

"But if you have nothing to create, then perhaps you create yourself."

To Paul...

What an incredible story! What an incredible book!
How you can feel, search for meaning, and look ...
How this book makes you understand and see,
That life is about searching and finding meaning to be
"the best me."

You are such an amazing, phenomenal man, Paul Lamb,
All you suffered, endured, survived, to be a new man.
God, always bless and watch over you!
Your story helps others to have strength, and believe too.

Life should be cherished; life is a prize.
Life would be enjoyed every moment, as one day,
one year, flies.
.With your story, you have touched my heart!
With every great book, you can begin a new start!

Paul, keep dong what you are doing! Your are truly a great
inspiration! Thank you for your beautiful and inspiring story!

Lucy Favero

Hi Paul,

… I just purchased your…. So far it is fascinating and the unusual style--part auto-biographical, part instructional, psychological text book, part philosophical inspiration--makes it an interesting read and guide.

I can promise you, your book will become a well loved companion over time--coffee stained, dog-eared, ragged--as all my prized possessions become. It is astounding to me that since 1996, you have not only dealt with what life dealt you, but you have also written this book, which will touch the hearts and minds and spirits of so many, who need to read about your journey in order to help them with theirs.

Meeting you, I was impressed by your openness of spirit--you will touch many, in ways you'll never know. Good Luck on the rest of you journey.

Susan Orpana

P erseverance

A ligns his life

U ltimate success

L earns about the truer meaning of life

L ets us all in on his personal story

A llows us to see a clearer view of our own life

M irrors what we can all be

B rightens our view on Exploring our own Iceberg

Ornella

CPSIA information can be obtained at www.ICGtesting.com
Printed in the USA
LVOW051832230413

330532LV00001B/5/P

9 781452 563145